Seeing More Colors

A GUIDE TO A RICHER LIFE

Michael S. Lewis M.D.

D1360913

Acknowledgments

One of the serendipitous joys of publishing this book is that I have benefited so much from the comments and insight of each of these individuals.

Leeann and Jack Ablin, Bobbi and Mel Adess, Gary Auerbach, Balbul and Vimel Bahuguna, Sarah Barnes, Sonia and Ted Bloch, Steve Brodsky, Sandy and the late John Callaway, Richie Campas, Jay Cohen, Doris and Howard Conant, Bonnie and Dennis Connolly, Alastair Davidson, Deb Donnelley, Laurel and Arthur Feldman, Michael Freed, Mick Friedberg, Ted and Sandra Friedberg, Jim and Sherry Friedberg, Rita and Tom Herskovits, Barbara and Raymond Kalmans, Arnie and Carol Kanter, Anita Kaplan, Morry and Dolores Kaplan, Elliott Krick, John Levin, Judy and Michael Lavin, Debi Lee, Beatrice Lewis, Hadley and Melanie Lewis, Shelly and Jeffrey Lewis, Greg Maggio, Bonnie and Martin Oberman, Eliezer Oberman, Michael and Margo Oberman, Lisa and William Oberman, Phil Paul, Norma and Peter Phillips, Anne Pizzi, Leonard Oshinski, Karen and David Sager, Larry Sartorious, Carol and Jim Schroeder, Gloria and Harry Schuman, Kate Searle, Art and Florence Shay, Richard Simon, Marilyn Susman, Jean and Geoff Tabin, Johanna and Julius Tabin, Nancy and Barry Waldman, Ken and Karen Waldman, June Waldman, Laurie Waldman, Sharon and Alan Waldman, Carol Walker, Susan and Steve Weiss, Bette and Tom Werlin, Eloise and Ernest Werlin, Alyssa Webb, Lynn Webb, Rollyn Wyatt, Ed Yastrow, Barbara Young, and Victor Zinn.

I am most grateful to Amy Martin of Four Colour Imports Ltd.; Roberta Rubin and Mary Joyce DiCola at The Book Stall at Chestnut Court in Winnetka, Illinois; Don Collins, Sue Tranchita, and Karen Hyzy at the Chicago Distribution Center; Steve Bennett of Authorbytes.com; and Alice Acheson of Acheson-Greub, Inc., each of whom has been most encouraging and supportive of my ventures into publishing.

Michal Janicki designed this book, the fourth we have worked on together. His star in the graphic arts field continues to rise.

Brandeis University generously granted permission to use photographs from their archives.

Several talented individuals have helped to edit the book. Deb Donnelley and Nancy Waldman, at an early stage of this project, helped to give it a needed focus and framework. Dr. Johanna Tabin, an eminent psychologist and psychoanalyst, added significant insight to the book, including deepening my understanding of Sigmund Freud's contributions to Abraham Maslow. Crissa Hiranaga is a chic and stylish woman, and these qualities are evident in her copy editing of this book. Susan Marvin kept saying, "Cut the fat," and worked tirelessly to help accomplish that, line by line. Aaron Feldman added numerous insights of his own to this book and helped to give it a consistent voice. Karen Zaworski is a talented professional. I am so grateful that she contributed her discerning eye as an artist and her elegance as a writer to this book.

My wife, Valerie Dewar Searle Lewis, enthusiastically and tirelessly added her inspiration and ideas to the book and should be considered co-author.

My daughter Melanie Dewar Lewis, also an editor, is one of the most well-read people I know. She forced me to question every premise in this book, which benefited from her dedication, sensitivity, and insight. She is a passionate reader and works at The Reading Clinic on the island of Maui where she helps transform struggling readers into competent, confident ones. To learn more about The Reading Clinic, please visit *thereadingclinicmaui.com*.

Profits from the sale of this book will be donated to the Himalayan Cataract Project, which is described in Chapter 5. The work of Geoffrey Tabin, M.D., may inspire you to help in the eradication of preventable blindness; contact the Himalayan Cataract Project at *cureblindness.org*.

Graphic design by Michal Janicki
with assistance from Johnny Mei

Printed in China by Everbest Printing Co.
through Four Colour Print Group, Ltd.,
Louisville, Kentucky

ISBN-13: 978-0-9790072-3-1

Dedicated to my wife,
Valerie Dewar Searle Lewis

"You are my soul's daily bread."
—*PABLO NERUDA*

Table of Contents

Introduction
Seeing More Colors: A Guide to a Richer Life

Roger Bannister breaks the four-minute mile

Conditions were far from ideal at Oxford, England's Iffley Road athletic track that day: cold and damp, with a fifteen mph crosswind and gusts nearly double that. Nonetheless, Roger Bannister, a twenty-five-year old university medical student, achieved the seemingly impossible: he broke the four-minute mile. Halfway around the world, in hot and humid Houston, Texas, I was an eleven-year old budding track athlete, awestruck at the news. May 6, 1954, was a day I will never forget.

Roger Bannister. England

"This summer I saw more colors than before."
—VINCENT VAN GOGH

Bog. Nova Scotia

The following Saturday morning, I paid the 9¢ admission fee to watch the race on *News of the World* at a nearby movie theatre. With 200 yards to go, Bannister had a final burst of energy and sprinted to the finish line. He then collapsed, utterly exhausted. With the announcer's first word, "Three…," pandemonium broke out among spectators at the race; in the theatre, the crowd cheered just as wildly.

A momentous event had happened, and I was elated. Something shifted inside of me. Though difficult to express, I understood that the possibilities of human achievement had suddenly expanded. When Sir Edmund Hillary reached the summit of Mount Everest and Neil Armstrong walked on the moon, I had a similar powerful reaction.

Fast forward to the early 1960s. Abraham Maslow, a professor of psychology at Brandeis University, where I was an undergraduate, formulated a theory to help explain the accomplishments of people like Roger Bannister.

Maslow postulated that such subjects do not simply accept circumstances that are handed to them. For example, before Roger Bannister, many scientists and physicians had concluded that breaking the four-minute mile barrier was physiologically impossible; astonishingly, within a few weeks of the event, several runners repeated the accomplishment.

Many years after his famous race, when reflecting on breaking the record, Bannister explained, "No longer conscious of my movement, I discovered a new unity with nature. I had found a new source of power and beauty, a source I never dreamt existed." Maslow studied similar descriptions of extraordinary life occurrences, and coined a term for them, *peak experiences.* He connected the seemingly unrelated phenomena of peak experiences and the idea that thoughts can create reality.

These were electrifying ideas for an insecure eighteen-year old like myself. For many, the high school and college years are a time for questioning, and the search for a meaningful path in life becomes intense. This was certainly true for me; discovering Maslow was, therefore, a salvation. Studying at the forefront of a new approach in psychology was exhilarating. Then, as now, I wondered: if it worked for those who were exceptional, why could it not work for the rest of us?

Maslow's importance to psychology

Who was Abraham Maslow?

Abraham Maslow's approach to psychology was simple, yet revolutionary. Instead of focusing on those with mental illnesses, as Sigmund Freud had done, he studied the emotionally healthiest people in our society. He called these people *self-actualized*. He concentrated on investigating their goals and actions in work, love, and play.

Before Maslow, Freud dominated the psychological universe with his studies of those with neurotic and psychotic illness. Freud concentrated on the unconscious; Maslow focused on the conscious. Maslow did not disavow Freud's theories, but instead built upon them. He believed that Freud "sold human nature short," and that we have "higher ceilings." Freud concentrated on the past. Maslow showed that the future is as important as the past, in terms of ideals, hopes, duties, and unrealized potential.

Just as Freud gained credibility as a scientist because he had been a well-trained neurologist prior to his change of direction to psychoanalysis, so Maslow's background in animal research and human abnormal psychology was a solid base from which to branch out into a more theoretical direction. I maintain that Maslow altered the landscape of how we perceive human nature as much as Freud had done for previous generations.

Abraham Maslow

Maslow's importance today

In many ways, these are the best of times. We live longer. We have more access to ideas and information. For many, food, education, services, travel, and material goods are available in remarkable quality and variety. Surrounded by such abundance, why are not more of us in a perpetual state of gratitude? Maslow can help us answer this question.

Maslow's ideas became the foundation for the movement known as *humanistic psychology*, which serves as a fundamental underpinning to today's study called *positive psychology*. Martin Seligman popularized the latter phrase in his 1998 address as president of the American Psychological Association, in which he reiterated Maslow's important emphasis upon increasing our potential.

Echoing Maslow's ideas, Seligman stated, "For the last half-century, clinical psychology has been consumed by a single topic only—mental illness." He further pointed out, "Psychology is not just the study of pathology, weakness, and damage; it is also the study of strength and virtue. Treatment is not just fixing what is broken; it is nurturing what is best."

"The world is but canvas to our imagination"
—HENRY DAVID THOREAU

A few important milestones

1908: Abraham Maslow born in Brooklyn, New York.

1934: Completes Ph.D. in psychology at University of Wisconsin-Madison, studying with Harry Harlow, the pioneer in animal social behavior, including mother-infant bonding in monkeys.

1937–1951: Teaches psychology at Brooklyn College, New York.

1941: Publishes *Principles of Abnormal Psychology*, based on Freud's theories of psychopathology, with Bela Mittelmann.

1951–1969: Heads psychology department at Brandeis University.

1954: Publishes *Motivation and Personality*, in which he formulates concepts of a hierarchy of needs, peak experiences, and self-actualization.

1970: Dies at age 62 after retiring to California.

Hierarchy of needs

Maslow conceptualized a hierarchy of needs on five levels:

- Physiological
- Safety
- Love, affection, and belongingness
- Esteem
- Self-actualization

Mankind's most basic and powerful needs are for physical survival, including oxygen, food, shelter, and sleep. When these needs are satisfied, the need for safety—particularly, feeling safe in one's own home—follows.

Once survival and safety needs are met, the needs for love and a feeling of belonging to a group become paramount, since we need to give and receive affection in order to feel part of the human family.

The next level in the hierarchy is the need for self-respect and self-esteem. A stable, high evaluation of oneself, together with being esteemed by others, leads to feelings of self-confidence, usefulness, and necessity in the world.

After advancing through this hierarchy of basic needs, one becomes less insecure, anxious, and selfish, and is then in a position to become self-actualized— that is, ready to fulfill one's potential.

Rice paddies. Vietnam

Mt. Everest. Nepal

Characteristics of the self-actualized

Nine characteristics described by Maslow enable the self-actualized to lead a more satisfying life. Each is fleshed out in a chapter of this book.

- Shaping reality
- Creativity
- Appreciating the moment
- Autonomy
- Focusing beyond oneself
- Humor and celebration
- Kinship
- Loving and being loved
- A propensity for peak experiences

What self-actualization is not

To some, the term *self-actualization* may suggest a specific state of being or a destination which one reaches, like arriving at the summit of a mountain, accompanied by feelings of serenity, ecstasy, and the transcendence of human problems.

This is not the case. It is important to recognize that self-actualization is a path one hopes to follow rather than a place where one arrives. It is a process of development that does not end.

All of us experience difficulties in everyday life. Emotional traumas and setbacks are common occurrences for each of us. Concerns about health, finances, family and friends, and the future of the planet never evaporate. To me, Maslow may have under-emphasized that the journey toward self-actualization has detours and road blocks.

Although many of the individuals mentioned in this book possess laudable qualities, Maslow would not necessarily consider them to be self-actualized. There-fore, rather than focus on specific people, I feel that it is more instructive to look at specific characteristics possessed by the self-actualized that can serve as a guide to living a more rewarding life.

One of the main criticisms of the concept of self-actualization has been that it leads to an overindulgent concern with one's own personal growth and fulfillment. Maslow's response: The self-actualized focus on people and problems outside of themselves; they do not operate in a vacuum, but always in relation to people and circumstances around them. They are able to balance independence of mind with strong ties to family and friends. They understand that everyone benefits through helping others. Maslow emphasizes that the ultimate expression of one's potential comes not only from personal achievement, but also from the capacity to transcend one's self in the service of others.

Maslow's importance in my life

Since Abraham Maslow has eloquently expressed his theories in several books and in numerous journal articles, and there is no shortage of biographical books, why write another book about him?

First, he was a mentor to me. I had a close personal relationship with him. He was instrumental in my decision to attend medical school. While at Brandeis, he said to me, "Someone is going to make significant contributions in the field. Why shouldn't it be you?"

"If you plan on being anything less than you are capable of being, you will probably be unhappy all the days of your life."
—ABRAHAM MASLOW

He continually pushed me to give my best effort. Success, I learned, meant that I would have to work harder than the other people surrounding me. Since reading Annie Dillard's book, *The Writing Life*, I often think of her description of how an author writes as a metaphor for life. "Aim for the chopping block. If you aim for the wood, you will have nothing. Aim past the wood, aim through the wood; aim for the chopping block." Maslow gave me the impetus to aim past the wood.

Secondly, it's exciting to be able to express Maslow's ideas not just in my own words, but also in the words of others, and in my photographic images from all seven continents.

His ideas have continued to capture my imagination for almost fifty years, infinitely expanding my own world, and helping me to lead a more enriched life. This book is an attempt to express my gratitude to Abraham Maslow.

Rooftops. Gaudaleste, Spain

Namib Desert. Namibia

Stones to step on

Looking at photographs and reading about ideas are only stepping stones to help guide us on our path.

"The map is not the territory."
—ALFRED KORZYBSKI

Taking the next step—applying Maslow's ideas toward one's life—is a challenge. Each of us is a work in progress.

"I am struggling every minute to live what I preach."
—MARIAN WRIGHT EDELMAN

In these pages I relate personal episodes of missteps as well as positive experiences. As painter and art teacher Robert Henri writes in *The Art Spirit*, "All any man can do is add his fragment to the whole... What he leaves is stones for others to step on or stones to avoid."

For me, accounts of "stones to avoid" can sometimes be as instructive as describing positive characteristics of the self-actualized. To illustrate this point, a much-loved family story: A cousin of mine redecorated her house using expensive wallpaper in her bedroom. Momentarily drawn from the room, she returned to discover her four-year-old daughter, Stephanie, together with her friend, Betsy, drawing on the newly-covered walls with indelible ink. After momentarily losing her southern-belle composure, my cousin regained control and asked her daughter what she was doing. Stephanie replied, "I was showing Betsy what not to do."

Just the essentials

Twenty years ago, a Chicago friend of mine was about to drive to Texas, my home state. He asked if he could bring anything back for me. I requested some Wolf Brand® chili, along with a case of Pearl beer in longneck bottles. (Those were the days before the discovery of the evils of high cholesterol.) In Texas, he walked up to the checkout counter of a convenience store with a case of Wolf Brand chili, a case of Pearl beer, and, for his own pleasure, a tin of Skoal's chewing tobacco. The cashier squinted briefly at the order and, in a thick Texan drawl, wryly pronounced, "Just the essentials."

This is not a book about how to become self-actualized in ten easy steps. At the same time, each story and quotation in this book captured my imagination, changed how I comprehend the world, and would fit my description of "just the essentials."

This book is not directed at those who are faced with significant emotional pain. (In such cases, professional consultation might be helpful.) Instead, it is directed at those coping with life's daily challenges, while knowing that a much greater sense of satisfaction is possible.

Michael Murphy, author of *The Future of the Body: Explorations into the Further Evolution of Human Nature*, states, "Human beings have enormous undeveloped potentials. We stand at the precipice of the next great evolutionary leap, a transformation of consciousness that has the power to change every aspect of our lives."

How can we tap into that transformation of consciousness, that extra power that pushed Roger Bannister to break a four-minute mile? I contend that Abraham Maslow's ideas can show each of us how to unlock our full potential, leading to a more rewarding life.

Wine jugs. Jerusalem, Israel

Buddhist monks playing. Punakha, Bhutan

1.

The Capacity to Shape Reality

Abraham Maslow observed that the self-actualized realize how much control they have over their own destiny. They are not ruled by their fears and anxieties, but have a clear sense of what is true and what is false. They focus their energies on productive activities.

Creating our own realities

"Being human is a surprise, not a foregone conclusion. A person has a capacity to create events," writes Abraham Joshua Heschel, a prominent twentieth-century Jewish theologian and philosopher, in his book, *Who Is Man?* Our external circumstances have little to do with the level of satisfaction we experience. Philip Brickman, Dan Coates, and Ronnie Janoff-Bulman, in a study published in the *Journal of Personality and Social Psychology* in 1978, determined that lottery winners tend to revert to their original personalities within six months of the radical change in their lives. This study shows there is little correlation between increased income and a greater sense of satisfaction once income is sufficient for basic needs.

"The real voyage of discovery consists not in seeing new landscapes but in having new eyes."
—MARCEL PROUST

In *The 7 Habits of Highly Effective People,* Stephen Covey maintains that the capacity to shape reality is enhanced by approaching issues proactively rather than reactively. Instead of "That is just the way I am," our response in the face of frustration could be, "I can choose a different approach." Covey emphasizes that ten percent of life is what happens to you—that which you have no control over—but ninety percent is decided by how you react. In other words, it is not the cards you are dealt, but how you play them.

Hadley Lewis

Courting an optimistic attitude

At the beginning of her senior year in high school, my daughter Hadley was elected captain of the field hockey, ice hockey, and softball teams. In autumn, during one of the first games of the field hockey season, she tore the anterior cruciate ligament in her knee. She had to undergo a painful surgery and months of physical therapy. The result was that she missed not just the rest of the field hockey and ice hockey seasons but also spring softball, as well as other once-in-a-lifetime, senior-year events. A few weeks after her surgery, she unselfconsciously remarked, "I have always been so fortunate. Nothing bad has ever happened to me." Admittedly, there are more serious conditions one might face than knee surgery. Nevertheless, how memorable it is when our own children remind us of life's important lessons.

It is easy to assume that circumstances are responsible for how we respond to a situation. Often you will hear someone say, "He made me feel bad." But no one can make us feel a certain way. We control our own reactions—to a great extent, things really are what we make of them.

"There is nothing either good or bad, but thinking makes it so."
—WILLIAM SHAKESPEARE

Choosing how to respond to circumstances

Henry Louis Gates, Jr., is an American literary critic, writer, and professor at Harvard University. In his autobiography, *Colored People*, he graphically portrays how differently his brother and his mother reacted to their individual circumstances.

Gates details poignantly how traumatic it was for his brother when people made promises to him that they did not keep. Gates writes, "Something happened to Rocky when the county school board lied to him. Something died inside, the part that spells the difference between hoping and doing, between casting wide or casting close, between wearing the horizon like a shawl around your shoulders or allowing it to choke you to death like one of those plastic dry cleaner bags that warn of suffocation in dark blue letters."

Gates contrasts this reaction with his mother's attitude toward other people. "She made the ignorant and ugly sound like scholars and movie stars, turned the mean and evil into saints and angels. She knew what people meant in their hearts, not what the world had forced them to become. She knew the way in which working too hard for paltry wages could turn you mean and cold, could kill the things that could make you laugh. She remembered the way you had hoped to be, not the way you actually were."

We can respond to circumstances by being crushed, as did Gates' brother, or we can respond by being uplifted, as did his mother. What is important to realize is that the choice is in our hands.

"One who will truly live life will pour life into every cranny, however cramped the space, shaping what is there rather than being shaped by it. It means roving imagination and daring thinking and ready laughter, and quick appreciation, and intense interest and wide observation."
—*PEARL BUCK*

Coping with fear

Elisabeth Kübler-Ross, M.D., was a psychiatrist famed for her work on death and dying. While on the oncology rotation during her psychiatry residency, Kübler-Ross encountered cancer patients who seemed to feel better after a particular hospital housekeeper had worked in their rooms.

Dr. Kübler-Ross was curious about these interactions and eventually confronted the housekeeper, who related this story: A few years previously, in the middle of winter, her four-year-old child had been sick. She took him to a nearby clinic, but they refused to treat him because she owed $6.50 on an old medical bill. She then had to take three buses to the county hospital, where she waited three more hours for her child to be examined. While waiting, her child died in her arms. She said that if she could survive that experience, she could survive just about anything.

She was no longer frightened of death. But some of the cancer patients on the ward were. By sharing her story and her encouraging manner, the housekeeper transmitted some of her strength of character to those frightened and unable-to-cope patients. Dr. Kübler-Ross called the woman the best teacher she had ever had, and spent the remainder of her professional career helping patients to re-shape their own realities regarding death. This story illustrates how our own interpretations of reality can powerfully affect our interactions with others.

Iceberg. Antarctica

"Every now and then a man's mind is stretched by a new idea or sensation, and never shrinks back to its former dimensions."
—OLIVER WENDELL HOLMES

Struggling to shape reality

When deciding how to react to a situation, being pro-active rather than reactive is excellent advice. That said, I know how difficult it can be to put this mantra into practice, as evidenced by experiences I had as a teenager and while in medical school.

At thirteen years old, I was a good athlete. I had come within one inch of a national broad jump record for my age group, won a three-state table tennis tournament, and bowled a 239 game. In my mind, I clearly was destined for greatness, but fate had a different idea. What I did not understand was that I had an early growth spurt. By age fourteen, my five feet and nine inches in height, as well as my glorious athletic achievements, were surpassed by many. The result was that I felt that my best years were already behind me. This was quite a lesson in humility. However, at that time, I was less concerned with shaping my own reality than with simply surviving my loss of self-esteem.

"Common sense is the collection of prejudices acquired by age eighteen."
—ALBERT EINSTEIN

Ten years later, during my second year of medical school, I still had not made much progress in learning how to shape my reality. I was complaining about my workload while at a family gathering. My complaint? Science was changing so rapidly, why should I have to memorize everything? My audience was my cousin Mick Friedberg,

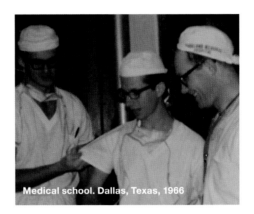

Medical school. Dallas, Texas, 1966

a distinguished psychologist and expert bridge player. I cited the example of how my biochemistry professor gave the same final exam questions year after year, though the field changed so quickly that the answers had changed too.

I was feeling rather sorry for myself. Several of my friends were already married, had an active social life, and seemed to have time to engage in interesting leisure pursuits. I, on the other hand, was simply drowning in chemical equations and obscure bacterial organisms. In response, several days later, a book arrived at my door with a note from cousin Mick: *It is all how you look at it.*

Gaining perspective

The book that cousin Mick sent me was *Unfair Advantage* by behavioral psychologist Tom Miller. In it, Miller invented a scale: from one to one hundred, what is the worst that could happen? The scale can be applied to all sorts of problems. One frame of reference might be bodily harm: the loss of a dominant arm might rank high—say eighty out of one hundred—but the loss of all four limbs might rank much higher, say ninety-five out of one hundred.

People do, of course, experience major tragedies like these. Tom Miller's scale is not intended to diminish the significance of these events; rather, it is intended to put lesser incidents in better perspective. When I read the book and considered Tom Miller's scale, I realized that my complaints about medical school were trivial— I estimated not more than five out of one hundred.

Mickey Rivers, a former center fielder for the New York Yankees, knew how to maintain perspective. During the 1978 season, he was badgered constantly by reporters over rumors that he was about to be traded. His response is instructive. "Ain't no use in worrying about things you don't have control over because if you ain't got no control over them, there's no use in worrying about them; and there ain't no sense in worrying about things you got control over, because if you got control over them, ain't no sense worrying." Identifying the problems we do not need to worry about and focusing on finding solutions to solvable problems are more productive uses of our time.

Losing perspective

Many years ago while in New Orleans, I paid a visit to my cousin Ted Friedberg, a well-respected professor of psychology. He wanted us to try our luck at the local casino. I am not much of a gambler, but he insisted.

That night, a construction worker from Mississippi won $15,000 at the craps table—an amount higher than his annual salary. Then his luck changed and he lost all of his winnings. Financially, he ended the day where he had begun. The next day there was a story about him in the *New Orleans Times-Picayune* newspaper. On his way home from the casino, he jumped off a bridge and committed suicide. He had no known history of mental illness.

Ted and I have reminded each other of that man's story many times. It is so easy to allow our unfulfilled expectations to cause us to lose perspective. Remembering this story after experiencing a painful setback has been helpful for me.

Courage under pressure

In the early 1980s my wife Valerie and I traveled to the former Soviet Union to assist refuseniks, Russian Jews who had applied to emigrate in order to find religious freedom but were refused. Often they were distinguished scientists or academicians who, after applying for a visa because of political repression, would lose their jobs, endure great financial difficulties, and face possible imprisonment. It was a great privilege to encounter some of the best, brightest, and bravest people we had ever met, each an inspiring example of how one might respond under extremely stressful circumstances. How precious is freedom! Our visit gave us a new awareness.

Young pioneers. Moscow, Soviet Union, 1984

Although we did not meet him at that time, refusenik Anatoly Sharansky was a particularly remarkable example of courage under appalling pressure. As recounted in his book *Fear No Evil*, Sharansky, upon being sentenced to thirteen years in a Siberian prison by a Moscow Court in 1978, declared, "Five years ago, I submitted my application to emigrate to Israel. Now I'm farther than ever from my dream. It would seem to be cause for regret. But it is absolutely otherwise. I am happy. I am happy that I lived honestly, at peace with my conscience. I never compromised my soul, even under the threat of death. I am happy that I helped people. . . . Now, when I am farther than ever from my people, from Avital (his wife), facing many arduous years of imprisonment, I say, turning to my people, my Avital: next year in Jerusalem."

As my wife and I witnessed in the Soviet Union at that time, many people do endure catastrophic traumas in their lives. Some are able to recalibrate their expectations and find fulfillment even in grim situations. It can take courage to keep things in perspective.

Reshaping reality

Each of us, even the luckiest, will face adversity. Some things just will not turn out as we hoped and planned. Under these circumstances, how can we maintain our perspective and shape our reality in a positive way? Few of us can react with the courage of Anatoly Sharansky or the housekeeper in the hospital who became Dr. Elisabeth Kübler-Ross's best teacher, but we can be inspired by their examples. When things are not going well, we can at least reassess ideas and habits that may have been useful in the past but are no longer effective. We can create new priorities.

"Once in a while it really hits people that they don't have to experience the world in the way they have been told to."
—ALAN KEIGHTLEY

Benjamin Disraeli stirringly said, "Most people die with their music still locked up inside them." We should not allow this to happen. The future does not have to be a replay of the past. We can create our own reality.

"There is a law in psychology that if you form a picture in your mind of what you would like to be, and you keep and hold that picture there long enough, you will soon become exactly as you have been thinking."
—WILLIAM JAMES

Boy with parakeets.
Iquitos, Peru.

2.

Creativity

Creativity is a characteristic shared by all of the self-actualized people Abraham Maslow studied. The self-actualized see life in terms of challenges that need creative solutions. It important to remember that each of us has the capacity to be creative.

Everyone is creative

For much of my life, I thought of creativity as destiny's rare gift visited upon a select few. I would look at these fortunate individuals with admiration and sometimes envy. I typically thought of creativity as applying only to purely artistic endeavors, such as composing music or painting a canvas, but innovative thinkers have broadened my definition.

The thought that each of us has the capacity to shape our daily lives in a creative way is encouraging. A person may run a business, build a motorcycle, or raise a family in a creative way. As Maslow affirmed, "A first-rate soup is better than a second-rate poem."

"Art is doing anything well. When the artist is alive, in any person, whatever his kind of work may be, he becomes inventive, searching, daring, self-expressing, creative. He becomes interesting to other people."
—*ROBERT HENRI*

Robert J. Sternberg, a former president of the American Psychological Association who became dean of the School of Arts and Sciences at Tufts University, is convinced that each of us has the capacity for creativity. In his book, *Wisdom, Intelligence, and Creativity Synthesized*, he defines creative intelligence as the ability to deal with challenging situations by drawing on existing knowledge and skills. He names creativity as one of the primary components of intelligence.

"Creative thinking involves imagining familiar things in a new light, digging below the surface to find previously undetected patterns, and finding connections among unrelated phenomena."
—ROGER VON OECH

Venice reflection. Venice, Italy

In 1997 I became an orthopedic consultant for the Chicago Bulls basketball team, and I was privileged night after night to observe the creative process in action: I watched Michael Jordan play. It was like watching an improvised ballet. He was an artist of surpassing grace on the court, continually creating moves to outmaneuver his defenders.

Michael Jordan was lucky enough to be both talented and creative. Talent is defined as a natural ability to do something well, while creativity is a way of thinking. The latter questions the status quo and tries to find unique solutions to problems. Supported by hard work, this is exactly what Michael Jordan did. Stephon Marbury recalled what it was like playing against him. "You ain't got no chance while Michael Jordan is playing. He overtakes people with his mind. He's not out there playing basketball with just his skills and his God-given talent. He's playing with his mind."

Michael Jordan, Chicago, Illinois

Redefining intelligence

Just as creativity should be defined more compre-
hensively, so should intelligence. Broader ideas about
creativity and intelligence highlight how differently
each of us develops. It is important to be more responsive
to these differences, and to remember that intelligence
is not a fixed commodity—it is constantly forming.

Howard Gardner, a psychologist at Harvard University,
writes about multiple forms of intelligence, quite independent from one another, with their own strengths and
constraints. He lists linguistic and logical-mathematical
intelligences, which are tested with the traditional
intelligence quotient (IQ) test, as well as musical, bodily-
kinesthetic, spatial, interpersonal, and intrapersonal
intelligences.

Gardner published these concepts more than twenty
years ago in *Multiple Intelligences: New Horizons in
Theory and Practice*, but he recently added naturalist
intelligence, which he sees as a greater sensitivity to
nature and one's place within it, and an ability to nurture
and grow things.

"Curiosity is one of the most permanent and certain characteristics of a vigorous intellect."
— SAMUEL JOHNSON

Daniel Goleman, a psychology professor at Rutgers University, further expands upon Gardner's concepts of interpersonal and intrapersonal intelligence. Goleman defines the subject of his book, *Emotional Intelligence,* as "the ability to monitor one's own and others' feelings and emotions, to discriminate among them and to use this information to guide one's thinking and actions." This includes the ability to detect and decipher emotions in faces and voices. He feels that emotional intelligence can be more important to a successful life than IQ.

Self-actualized people tend to see the positive in a situation. At the same time, they understand that managing negative emotions is essential. Goleman calls this a key aspect of emotional intelligence. In addition, being aware of our own strengths and weaknesses allows us to cultivate the former and fortify the latter.

Sardine boats. Essaouira, Morocco

"Most men live whether physically, intellectually or morally, in a very restricted circle of their potential being. They make use of a very small portion of their possible consciousness and of the soul's resources in general. Much like a man who out of his whole bodily organism can get into the habit of using and moving only his little finger."
—WILLIAM JAMES

"A child's mind is fresh and new and beautiful, full of wonder and excitement."
—RACHEL CARSON

Young girl. Soweto, South Africa

Dreaming of infinite possibilities

"Anything you can imagine is real."
— PABLO PICASSO

Many children start by exploring the world with unfettered imaginations. A class of first graders, when asked if they are artists, will all respond positively. Yet by the time they reach the eighth grade, almost no child feels this way. Our goal as we grow older should be to maintain our child-like sense of curiosity.

"Every child is an artist. The problem is how to remain an artist once he grows up."
— PABLO PICASSO

Imagination is a vital part of creativity. Beginning when I was six years old, Professor Joseph Werlin, a relative and a university sociology professor, began taking students on summer tours of Europe. When he returned, he brought coins from the countries he toured and distributed them among my cousins and me. The coins ignited my imagination and I dreamed of visiting castles on the Rhine River, sailing the Mediterranean, and viewing royal pageants in England. This prompted me to learn more about foreign countries in the Encyclopedia Britannica and to develop a life-long interest in travel and photography. Children surprise parents all the time by retelling stories years later—stories that the parents thought had never registered in the first place. One never knows how a small word or deed can reverberate.

"Without leaps of imagination or dreaming, we lose the excitement of possibility. Dreaming, after all, is a form of planning."
— GLORIA STEINEM

African tulip tree. Maui, Hawaii, USA

Understanding how the creative process works can help us to maintain our childlike imaginations. Authors Daniel Goleman, Paul Kaufman, and Michael Ray write of four stages of creativity in their book, *The Creative Spirit*. The first is preparation, which is the gathering of information. The second is incubation, which involves mulling over information and allowing time for it to gel. The third is illumination, in which a breakthrough occurs, sometimes suddenly and spontaneously. The last, translation, frames the insight in concrete terms and tests it for accuracy. Samuel Taylor Coleridge poetically illustrates the stages of incubation and illumination. "What if you slept? And what if in your sleep, you dreamed? And what if in your dream, you went to heaven and there plucked a strange and beautiful flower? And what if when you awoke, you had the flower in your hand?"

Benjamin Franklin, a founding father of the United States, used his imagination to improve not only his life, but also the lives of each of us. He understood that the future does not have to be a replay of the past. He saw sick people and founded a hospital. He saw a fire and created the fire department. He saw people needing an education and founded a university. It takes courage to think creatively, but look at the results in Franklin's case!

"It takes courage to be creative. Just as soon as you have a new idea, you're in the minority of one."
—*E. PAUL TORRANCE*

Exploring new arenas

We all have boundaries within which we feel comfortable. It is difficult to think outside of our comfort zone, and even more difficult to act outside of it. Yet part of creativity is exploring new arenas. Sometimes this can yield rich rewards.

On one occasion in particular, I pushed against my personal comfort zone and it led to a positive result. I self-published a book of photographs. The learning curve was steep, with numerous production steps, including organizing material, designing the layout, publishing, and marketing. This project was quite challenging. I had no idea whether my book would fail or succeed, but I gave it my best effort. Fortunately, the book seemed to genuinely affect many people on a deep level, which was an unexpected joy.

"I will act as if what I do makes a difference."
—*WILLIAM JAMES*

On other occasions, expanding into new arenas yielded more mixed results. A few years ago, I joined the boards of several organizations, including a Chicago museum, a suburban theatre group, and my local synagogue, as well as the executive committee at my primary hospital. I found that, although my input was generally helpful, I had no special talent in those directions. Ultimately, I moved on to other projects. However, if I had not tried, I would never have known whether or not I could have made an impact. It can be a challenge to know if one needs to give a project more of an effort, or if one's energies are better applied elsewhere. Understanding one's strengths and trying to match them to a project is one place to start. In any case, it was helpful to view these activities as enjoyable and life-enhancing detours rather than as failures.

"Rowing harder does not help if the boat is headed in the wrong direction."
—KENICHE OHMAE

Thinking beyond defeat

Abraham Lincoln did not allow himself to be defined by his defeats. He persevered in spite of losing an election for the legislature, failing in business, and being defeated in Senate runs in both 1854 and 1858. Yet in 1860, he was elected president of the United States, and is considered to be one of our greatest presidents by most historians.

"We see reality through a narrow window, but the doors of perception are infinite."
—ALDOUS HUXLEY

The Treasury. Petra, Jordan

Michael Jordan was not always successful. As a sophomore in high school, he was cut from the varsity basketball team. He was unsuccessful in his attempt to become a major league baseball player, and he missed many potential game-winning shots as a professional basketball player. However, one reason that he is considered by many to be the greatest basketball player in history is that he was not afraid of a new challenge. He was not afraid of failure.

"You always miss 100% of the shots you don't take."
—WAYNE GRETSKY

Recalibrating goals

In the late 1970s I was one of the first orthopedic surgeons in the country to perform arthroscopic knee surgery. I gave lectures, wrote articles, and even invented an arthroscopic instrument still used today. Patients came from several Midwest states for treatment. I thought this status quo would last forever. However, other orthopedic surgeons quickly learned the technique, and my competitive advantage rapidly diminished.

Simply maintaining the status quo was not sufficient then, or now. I should have remembered how Roger Bannister pushed himself to reach previously unobtainable goals. I should have set my goals higher then. I would like to think that I remain at the forefront of my field because of learning from my experiences.

"The greatest danger for most of us lies not in setting our aim too high and falling short, but in setting our aim too low and achieving our mark."
—MICHELANGELO

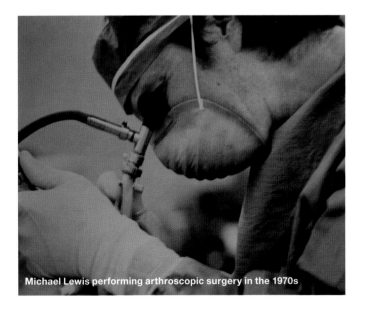

Michael Lewis performing arthroscopic surgery in the 1970s

By not giving a project your best shot, you have a ready excuse if it does not work out. You can claim that you would have succeeded if you had tried harder. But hard work can, indeed, win out over pure talent. I have observed several athletes who were blessed with extraordinary talent, but were not as successful as their less-gifted peers simply because they did not push themselves as hard. In my experience, giving one hundred percent effort to a project often unleashes energy that one did not know one possessed.

"The only way to discover the limits of the possible is to go beyond them to the impossible."
—ARTHUR C. CLARK

3.

Appreciating the Moment

Abraham Maslow described the self-actualized as having the capacity to appreciate life's daily activities as fresh experiences. They treat the moment-to-moment business of living with awe, pleasure, and wonder. Frequently recurring miracles of life—sunsets, flowers, your lover's smile—are still miracles. Like all of the characteristics of the self-actualized, it is important to remember that each of us can cultivate this appreciation.

"There are only two ways to live your life. One is as though nothing is a miracle. The other is as though everything is a miracle."
—*ALBERT EINSTEIN*

Missing the moment

Recently, *The Washington Post* ran the following story: A man sat at a metro station in Washington, D.C., on a cold January morning and started to play the violin. He played for forty-five minutes. Since it was rush hour, thousands of people went through the station. While the musician played, only six people stopped and stayed for a while.

The violinist was Joshua Bell, one of the best musicians in the world today. He played six intricate pieces by Johann Sebastian Bach with a violin worth $3.5 million. Two days before, Bell's concert in Boston had sold out. One of the world's best musicians was playing some of the best music ever written. Of course, there are many possible explanations why more people did not stop. Many people may have loved the music, but were late for work or other important engagements. Others may have been too cold or ill to linger and listen. Apart from people's motivation to simply pass by, the story remains a powerful metaphor for the importance of seeing with fresh eyes and being in the moment.

Shoes. Fez, Morocco

"The world will never starve for wonder, but only for want of wonder."
—G. K. CHESTERTON

When am I going to get there?

Several years ago I was traveling to a seminar on meditation and environmental awareness. It was to take place on the island of St. John in the Virgin Islands. I flew from a wintry Chicago to St. Thomas, and from there took a boat to St. John. It was early evening, and a magical sunset filled the sky, against a backdrop of mountain-fringed Caribbean islands. Upon boarding the boat, a woman also attending the retreat asked impatiently, "When are we going to get there?"

"This is now. Now is. Don't postpone till then.
Spend the spark of iron on stone. Sit at the head
of the table. Dip your spoon in the bowl. Seat
yourself next to your joy and have your awakened
soul pour joy."
—*RUMI*

I try very hard to be in the moment, but it has been a struggle to overcome years of asking, "When am I going to get there?" Throughout much of my medical training, my classmates and I were future oriented. Imagining what it would be like to be a "real doctor" made it easier to spend those long hours in the anatomy lab. In the medical field, it is common to remain in this future-oriented cycle. For example, as a medical student one might be thinking, "I cannot wait to become a resident in my specialized area." When one became a resident this would change to, "I cannot wait to get into the real world." Once in practice, one's thought might become, "I cannot wait to become more established." Later this became, "I cannot wait to retire." These examples might seem like hyperbole, but I have heard each many times. I find it quite disturbing. Of course, there are many who feel privileged to be in the medical field, and who enjoy each stage of the process.

Being in the moment

I attended medical school from 1964 until 1968, followed by a year of internship in San Francisco. After four years of the medical school grind, I experienced a new-found sense of freedom. I intended not just to focus on the future, but also to learn how to appreciate the moment.

In 1969, during my internship year, I worked hard, and I played hard. I lived one block from Haight and Ashbury streets in San Francisco, where the effects of the 1967 "summer of love" still echoed. I threw myself into the local scene. On weekends I would attend concerts by Janis Joplin, Jefferson Airplane, the Grateful Dead, Ravi Shankar, and Miles Davis. In addition to music, I tried new and different kinds of clothes, food, attitudes, and beliefs. I rejoiced in my rediscovery of the outdoors: I skied at Lake Tahoe, sailed in San Francisco Bay, and hiked among the redwood trees in Muir Woods. After all, it was the Age of Aquarius. Astrologers explained to us that we were entering a time of love, light, and humanity.

"Don't laugh at youth for his affectations; he is only trying on one face after another to find a face of his own."
—*LOGAN PEARSALL SMITH*

My mind was expanded by many profound philosophical discussions, though my main contribution to many of these was adding meaningful insights such as, "Far out!" and "Hea--vy." In spite of my simple vocabulary, I was learning how to appreciate the moment.

Michael Lewis and Ravi Shankar. Big Sur, California

The grass is always greener

One episode in particular helped me to see myself more clearly from the perspective of others. During a trip to England in the early 1960s, I briefly dated a young woman who was a lead singer in the D'Oyly Carte Opera Company, which traveled the world performing Gilbert and Sullivan operas. When they performed in San Francisco in 1969, she invited me to the cast party after the show. I looked around with envy at the cast members; in my eyes they led glamorous lives compared to my status as a medical intern. Yet when several cast members discovered that I was a physician, their reaction was, "You are so fortunate. We never have time to stay in one place long enough to enjoy it."

"There are two things to aim at in life: first, to get what you want; and, after that, to enjoy it. Only the wisest of mankind achieve the second."
—LOGAN PEARSALL SMITH

After my internship year in San Francisco, I spent the next four years as a resident in orthopedic surgery in New York City. I moved on to new worlds of possibility. Seeing myself from the perspective of members of the D'Oyly Carte Opera company, better understanding how to live in the moment, and internalizing new experiences helped me to begin to find my own voice.

Seeing people with fresh eyes

When my daughter Melanie was three years old, she taught me a valuable lesson about how to see people with fresh eyes. We were at the beach, and nearby a woman was shuffling along the sand. She appeared to be carrying the weight of the world on her stooped shoulders. Melanie, who had never seen her before, spontaneously asked, "Are you a princess?" The woman thought it over, and suddenly her posture became much more upright. "Why, yes, I am!" she responded, and continued her walk along the beach with a much livelier step.

"Words are of course the most powerful drug used by mankind."
—RUDYARD KIPLING

Humpback whale. Antarctica

"*The present is the wave that explodes over my head, flinging the air with particles at the height of its breathless unroll.*"

—*ANNIE DILLARD*

In order to see someone with fresh eyes, imagine that you are seeing an old friend for the first time, or that you may never see that friend again.

"If you always assume the man sitting next to you is the Messiah waiting for some simple human kindness, you will soon come to weigh your words and watch your hands. And if he chooses not to reveal himself in your time – it will not matter."
—DANNY SIEGEL

Sometimes when my energy lags, at the end of a day of seeing patients, I think of Siegel's advice. I look at the next patient, think maybe he or she is the Messiah, and I am reinvigorated.

Seeing your surroundings with fresh eyes

There are always ways to see with fresh eyes. For example, placing a familiar object in a new environment gives one a sense of renewal. It is remarkable how much a work of art changes when framed differently, or hung in a new location. In many Japanese homes, a fresh perspective is achieved when each of a family's art objects is only displayed for a month at a time.

Wildflowers, Israel

Looking at familiar objects as if you had never seen them before can engender a surprising reaction.

"People from another planet without flowers would think we must be mad with joy the whole time to have such things about us."
— IRIS MURDOCH

Claude Monet repeatedly painted haystacks. Each painting portrays a different time of day or a different season. It strikes me not only that he was trying to capture a different moment in time, but also that he was seeing a completely new world in each haystack.

Seeing activities with fresh eyes

Phil Jackson coached the Chicago Bulls basketball team
for nearly a decade. During his last two championship
years with Chicago (the 1997-1998 and 1998-1999
seasons), I worked with the team as an orthopedic
consultant. Phil was an avid reader, and he and I enjoyed
exchanging and discussing books with each other.
One was his own book, *Sacred Hoops*. In it, he eloquently
conveys the importance of being in the here and now,
with such expressions as "being fully engaged" and
"the joy of the dance."

Jackson grew up in North Dakota, where his ideas about
how to play basketball were influenced by the philosophy
of the neighboring Lakota Sioux. He translated their
ideas into sports-applicable expressions: Don't hold back.
Play the way you live your whole life–with your whole
heart and soul.

In several interviews, Michael Jordan credited Jackson
with keeping the Bulls' team centered and in the
moment. Through Jackson, Jordan said, the players
learned to find peace within themselves, even amid
the noise. This allowed the team to weigh options,
create solutions, and retain the equanimity required
to execute them.

Phil Jackson, moments after winning the NBA championship.
Chicago, 1998

*"Give it all. Give it now. Spend it now. Anything
you do not give freely and abundantly becomes lost
to you. You will open your safe and find ashes."*
—ANNIE DILLARD

Increasing our awareness of each moment

Our best moments occur when we are noticing what is happening in the here and now. In *Fly Fishing through the Midlife Crisis*, Howell Raines captures a moment of peace and serenity when he compares a particular fishing trip to being like "…opening day at the garden of Eden."

Fishing gear. New Zealand

It is so easy to be distracted. Who would have thought that a common cause of visits to emergency rooms in New York City on Sunday mornings is a knife wound from slicing a bagel?

"When we pay attention, whatever we are doing—whether it be cooking, cleaning or making love—is transformed. We begin to notice details and textures that we never noticed before; everyday life becomes clearer, sharper, and at the same time more spacious."
—RICK FIELDS

How can we teach ourselves to be more in the here and now? Jon Kabat-Zinn, a founding director of the Center for Mindfulness in Medicine at the University of Massachusetts Medical School, offers a simple exercise. Hold one raisin in your mouth and concentrate on it for several minutes. Pay attention to the taste. Pay attention to the speed at which you eat it. With a simple act like this, one can increase the awareness of the senses—and appreciate the moment with clarity.

Great Egret. Amazon River, Peru

"The quieter you become, the more you can hear."
—*BABA RAM DAS*

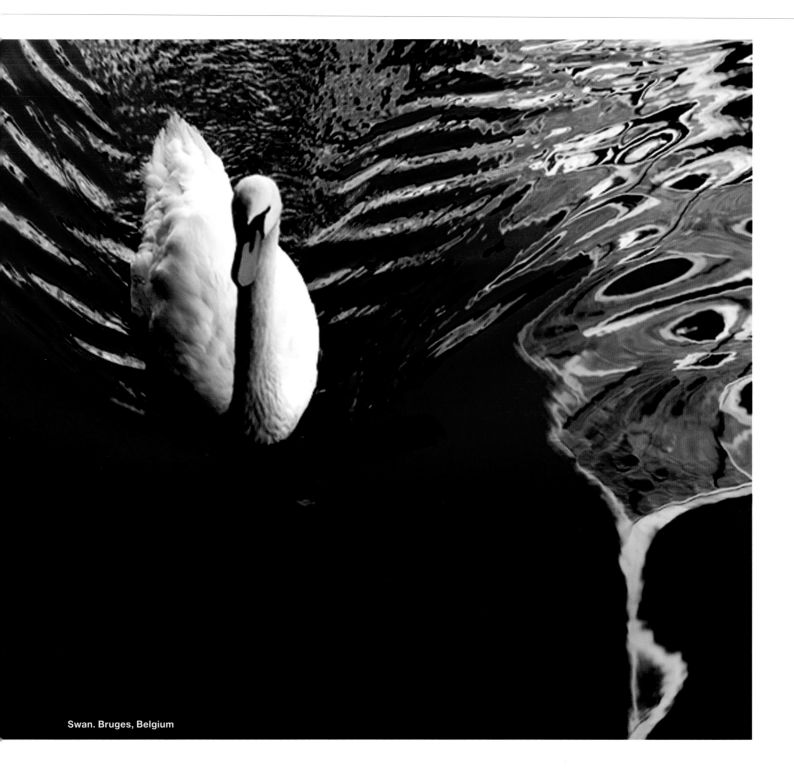

Swan. Bruges, Belgium

"Beauty and grace are performed, whether or not we will or sense them. The least we can do is to try to be there."
—*ANNIE DILLARD*

African fish eagle. Botswana

4.

Autonomy

According to Abraham Maslow, the self-actualized are autonomous and stick to their own interpretation of a situation rather than relying on the assessments of others. How is autonomy manifest in action? The self-actualized are more likely to set their own personal agendas. They do not rebel for the sake of rebellion but are willing to defy the crowd when necessary. Less inclined to judge themselves against someone else's capabilities, beauty, skills, or other attributes, they are more likely to value their own unique qualities.

While being faithful to their own ideas, the self-actualized maintain respect for the right of others to have their own opinions. Their autonomy avoids crossing the line to arrogance. The self-actualized not only think independently, but also act on their own thoughts.

"To be nobody but myself—in a world which is doing its best, night and day, to make you everybody else—means to fight the hardest battle which any human being can fight, and never stop fighting."
—e.e. cummings

Standing up for what is right

The self-actualized are not only independent thinkers but also willing to take action when necessary. The following story is about my mother's brother, Uncle Whiz (a nickname for Isadore). Whereas another person might keep his opinions to himself rather than risk hurting his business, my uncle Whiz was always outspoken, particularly when the rights of others were concerned.

The story takes place in Galveston, Texas, in the early 1960s, when racial segregation was a part of life. Uncle Whiz was a young optometrist, building his practice one eye exam at a time. A big, burly Texan came into Whiz's office, and found himself waiting in line behind an African-American woman. When Whiz asked the woman to come into his office, the man interrupted with, "Hey, are you going to take that woman before you take me?" The hostile look on the man's face, and his tone, made his meaning unmistakable. Whiz took the lady back into his office, asked her to wait, and returned to where the big guy was standing. Whiz, who stood 5 feet, 7 inches and weighed 150 pounds dripping wet, told this intimidating fellow, "Listen, you no-good racist, I want you to get the hell out of my office right now, and if you have any friends, I wish you'd tell them to stay out of here, too." The man left but returned a couple of weeks later. Whiz saw his life flash before him at the realization that the racist man was fully capable of killing him. Amazingly, the fellow apologized.

Failing to take action

Knowing the right thing to do and actually doing it are two different things. Lisa Nichols, an author and motivational speaker, tells the following story in her book, *No Matter What!* One day, a man walked past a house and saw a little old lady rocking in her chair, a little old man reading the paper as he rocked next to her, and a dog lying on the porch between the two, moaning as if he were in pain. As he passed, the man wondered silently what the dog was moaning about.

The next day, he walked past the house again. He saw the old couple rocking in their chairs and the dog lying between them, making the same pained sound.

On the third day, to his distress, he saw the same scene: the little old lady rocking, the little old man reading, and the dog in his spot, moaning piteously. He could not stand it anymore.

"Excuse me, ma'am," he called out to the old woman, "what's wrong with your dog?"

"Oh, him?" she said. "He's lying on a nail."

Confused by her reply, the man asked, "If he's lying on a nail and it hurts, why doesn't he just get up?"

The little old lady smiled and said in a sweet, grandmotherly tone, "Well, honey, it hurts just enough for him to moan about it, but not enough for him to move yet."

Remembering this story has saved me a lot of emotional wear and tear.

Halong Bay, Vietnam

"You have a blue guitar, you do not play things
as they are." The man replied, "Things as they are,
are changed upon a blue guitar."
—WALLACE STEVENS

Seeking approval from others

One of life's challenges is to know when to accept advice from others and when to be guided by one's own instincts. There is no simple formula. A pivotal experience in my life happened when I was a senior in high school in Houston, Texas. The experience challenged my notion of self and was very painful to me. I was president of a Jewish youth group, and it was time to elect the next year's officers. Prior to the election, our rabbi, a man I greatly admired, pulled me aside and told me to make sure Charlie was elected as president. I did not ask why, as Charlie was admired by the rabbi and everyone else. He was an elegant but somewhat aloof young man and had been slated for the office by the nominating committee, so it did not occur to me that there would be a problem. However, on voting day, a classmate named Steve—down-to-earth, popular, and a close friend—won, fair and square. Nonplussed, I did not follow my own instincts, which were to declare Steve the new president. Instead, I suggested a re-vote and convinced the other members to vote instead for Charlie. Steve and his family, close friends of my family, were quite upset, and with good reason. I had done what I was told to do by an adult I respected. The result was that I had alienated someone I cared about, and I felt terrible.

Although many people might have recovered quickly from this awkward situation, for me it led to a major identity crisis. While growing up, my actions were geared typically toward gaining approval from others; that approach was ineffective in this situation. The result was personal confusion and turmoil. I should have stood my ground, but I did not. I needed to develop my own voice, to listen to it, and to be more willing to be guided by my own instincts.

Inspirational speakers often will tell us to "follow our heart." How do we learn to do this? It is no coincidence that each of the self-actualized described by Maslow have had considerable life experience. It usually takes many years' worth of learning experiences—sometimes painful—to understand ourselves well enough to take this advice.

What can we do in the interim? I have found it helpful to take as much time as possible to make important decisions. Instead of an immediate yes or no, I try to give myself time "to sleep on it." Things in the I-cannot-live-without-it category sometimes seem less important the next day. Also, I remember the acronym H.A.L.T., which stands for hungry, angry, late, and tired, and I try not to make consequential decisions in these circumstances.

What if an immediate decision is required? I can at least step back and ask how my decision might look to a mentor whom I respect. What if my choice will not affect the result? I can in any case state my position, especially if it is an unpopular one.

"No man will live my life for me, no one will think my thoughts for me or dream my dreams."
—*ABRAHAM JOSHUA HESCHEL*

Each of us takes a different path while learning to think for ourselves. Several years ago I had a patient in my office whose problem was immediately curable. As she was leaving the office, she turned to me and, in a demanding way, said, "Is that all?" I was puzzled by her reaction and replied, "I am not sure what you mean. You are one of the lucky ones. You are cured." She hesitated, and then she apologetically responded, "Yes, you are right, but I have just completed an assertiveness training class!"

Assertiveness training is one way to help people develop life skills, including speaking up when necessary. This can lead to becoming more autonomous, but must be balanced with controlling one's anger. In *The Cultural Animal: Human Nature, Meaning and Social Life*, Roy F. Baumeister explains that simply expressing anger is not beneficial. It is helpful only when it is accompanied by constructive problem-solving designed to address the source of the anger.

Koala. New South Wales, Australia

"The things that make you different, that's where your poetry is."
—*STEPHEN COVEY*

Balancing individualism with family and friends

Being autonomous is important, but I have found it a challenge to balance my own personal and professional activities with being with family and friends. Observing how other cultures, as well as previous generations, have dealt with this issue is instructive.

A few years ago, a study comparing relative levels of satisfaction in different countries was published; both Ghana and the United States were included. Although its per capita income is a fraction of that in the United States, Ghana was higher on the satisfaction scale. I happened to be training a Ghanaian resident physician at the time, and I asked him for his explanation. He responded by relating a recent phone call that he had received from a friend back home. His friend inquired, "Is it really true that before you visit someone in the United States, you must call them first to get permission?" When the resident answered in the affirmative, his friend replied, "You must come home immediately. How can you live in such a place?"

"Being neighborly" used to mean dropping in on friends. Now, for many in the United States, it often means respecting their privacy by leaving them alone.

Women at the market. Kumasi, Ghana

Women at a festival, Bali

When my wife and I were in Bali, Indonesia, we had a guide who was a young father in his thirties. He proudly stated that he had just returned from a one-month vacation with his family, spent doing what gave him more joy than anything else imaginable: he constructed his father's grave. The family and community are paramount in Bali. It is common to have several generations of a family living together in the same compound. Families belong to both clans and cooperative groups of neighbors called *banjars,* who assist each other at festivals, family gatherings, and at times of crisis. This model has worked for centuries.

It is easy to understand the advantages of seeking opportunities wherever one finds them, such as accepting a job far from family roots, but there is a high price to pay. When my parents were growing up, there were always relatives living with them. My parents both came from large families that emigrated to the United States from eastern Europe and settled in Houston, Texas. There are countless family stories about more settled members helping new arrivals to become established. The actions of the previous generations helped foster very close relationships in my generation. To this day, I have cousins who are like brothers and sisters.

In contrast, a considerable part of the mythology of the United States is centered around the exploits of heroic individuals, from the entrepreneur who starts his own company to the lone cowboy who explores the open range. A book that I have read many times through the years, Henry David Thoreau's *Walden* emphasizes the importance of discovering things on your own.

Psychology professor David G. Myers writes in *The Pursuit of Happiness*, "We need to balance me-thinking with we-thinking." The self-actualized, as well as many members of my own family and friends, appear to have achieved this balance. It continues to be a struggle for me, but I find it helpful to remember Ralph Waldo Emerson's philosophy: The only gift is a portion of thyself.

"The journey is uniquely yours, no one else's. In the trajectory between birth and death, a human life is lived. No one escapes the adventure. We only work with it differently."
—JON KABAT-ZINN

Resisting conformity

Part of being autonomous includes questioning conventional wisdom and looking at issues from a viewpoint different than one's own. Endel Tulving, a world authority on human memory function and professor at Yale University, told his undergraduates, "Just because a lot of people believe something does not make it true. Further, you should be very suspicious of it."

Our institutions encourage conformity in an attempt to mold us into more predictable members of society. Like a fish that may not realize it is swimming in water, we often do not notice when our intellectual and emotional agendas are co-opted by others. A rigid ideology can be a substitute for our own thoughts.

The media bombard us daily with ideas and images suggesting how to think and what to buy. Finances, to a great extent, affect "the news." For example, "If it bleeds it leads" is a well-known theme on the nightly news. It is less expensive to show images of a burning building than to conduct an intensive investigation of corruption in government. Also, studies show that images of fire increase our adrenalin level, which leads to a sharper focus on the advertisers' products.

Every year *New York* magazine lists the ten most powerful people in New York City. Typically, the news editor of the *New York Times* is always high on the list. Initially, I thought that the editorial page editor would be more powerful, but a newspaper reporter friend explained that the person who decided which stories would appear on the front page was more important than the editor who opined about those stories. The former set the agenda. Front page newspaper stories may seem more subtle and benign than violent images on television. In fact, both illustrate how insidiously our thoughts can be directed by others.

"Learning rules is useful, but it is not education. Education is thinking—looking for yourself and seeing what is there—not what you got told was there."
—WILLIAM LEAST HEAT-MOON

Bulletin board with weekly newspaper. Suchow, China, 1982

Fewer words, more action

While I was an undergraduate at Brandeis University, well-known leaders in various fields would come to the university to discuss their lives and work. Bruno Bettelheim, a psychologist known for his work on autism, spoke to us during the time of the freedom rides in the civil rights movement. His speech forcefully underscored the importance of personal action.

During the question-and-answer period, one student suggested to Professor Bettelheim that the professor should go on a freedom ride. The student received more than he had anticipated as an answer. The professor became red in the face and, although a relatively short man, seemed suddenly to grow several feet taller. He walked off the stage, stood over the questioner, and shouted at him, "Don't you tell me what to do! I'm doing what I think is important. Instead of making suggestions to others, why aren't you on a freedom ride right now?"

It was one of the most unforgettable and meaningful moments in my college career. I am still trying to learn that powerful lesson in autonomy from Bruno Bettelheim: less unsolicited advice to others and more personal action.

"It's not the same to talk of bulls as to be in the bullring."
—*PHIL JACKSON*

5.

Focusing beyond Oneself

Abraham Maslow observed that all self-actualized people have a mission in life which focuses on problems outside of themselves. Feeling blessed with an abundance of personal gifts, they are generous toward others and desire to create an environment in which others can thrive. This includes finding a vocation that gives one the opportunity to make the world a better place. It is important to remember that each of us has a certain skill set with which we can make a unique contribution.

Generosity and kindness

"My religion is kindness."
—*DALAI LAMA*

One of my favorite stories on the theme of generosity and kindness is told by Nobel Laureate Elie Wiesel. A rabbi and sage known as the Tzaddik, or wise man, of Nevirov had a habit of disappearing during the time of the holiday of Rosh Hashanah. Everyone knew that he went to heaven at that time "to take care of a few things." A neighbor was skeptical and was determined to follow the rabbi. He observed that the rabbi rose early, dressed like a peasant, chopped down a tree, and split it into logs. Then, disguised as a seller of wood, he went to the home of a poor, sick widow. She told him that she could not afford his wood, but he proceeded to light the fire and told her not to worry about payment. After observing all of this, the neighbor became the rabbi's most devoted follower. When asked if the rabbi went to heaven during the high holidays, he no longer sneered, but answered, "To heaven? No, higher."

"Shall we make a new rule of life from tonight: always be a little kinder than is necessary."
—SIR JAMES BARRIE

The literature of positive psychology presents several studies that show that helping others increases one's likelihood of leading a more satisfying life. It's a win-win situation. The more one gives, the more one receives.

As Martin Luther King, Jr. often preached, "Everybody can be great, because anybody can serve. You only need a heart full of grace, a soul generated by love."

Giving joyfully

Abraham Joshua Heschel sums up the importance of giving joyfully in *God in Search of Man*: "It has been said that the joy with which a deed is done is more precious than the deed itself. The good without the joy is a good half done; and the love and delight with which we do the good and the holy are the test of our spirit."

"There are those who give with joy, and that joy is their reward."
—KAHLIL GIBRAN

I happily conspired with my two daughters, both of whom live far away, to surprise my mother, Beatrice Lewis, at her home on one of her recent birthdays. I received a perfect gift in return: the joy quotient in the house really spiked.

Birthday surprise. Houston, Texas

"Let the heavens dance for joy and let the earth reverberate with glee."
—PSALMS

Eradicating preventable blindness

Self-actualized people know that one's life is a gift to be shared. They devote themselves to making the world better for others. Geoffrey Tabin's work exemplifies this principle. Dr. Tabin is co-founder, along with Dr. Sanduk Ruit from Nepal, of the Himalayan Cataract Project, an organization with the goal of eradicating preventable blindness worldwide. He not only performs surgery, but also teaches local doctors and nurses cataract surgery techniques. Together they have returned sight to more than five hundred thousand people. I was most fortunate to accompany Dr. Tabin to Ghana in 2007. During that two-week visit, he and his team performed more than four hundred cataract surgeries. People from remote areas, with little or no access to health care, underwent surgery, then were fed and housed overnight before being re-examined the next morning, all for no charge to them. People who had been blind or who had had minimal vision were able to walk away unaided, excited at the prospect of seeing their children and grandchildren— sometimes for the first time.

"I have sometimes seen what other men have only dreamed of seeing."
—ARTHUR RIMBAUD

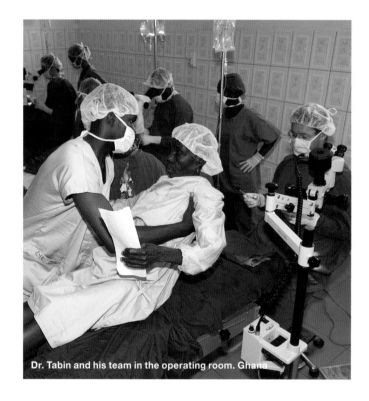

Dr. Tabin and his team in the operating room. Ghana

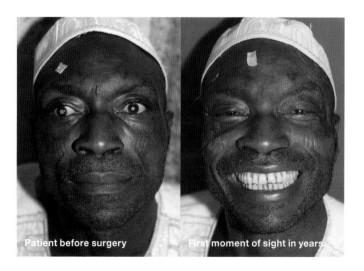

Patient before surgery   First moment of sight in years

Land mine victims. Siem Riep, Cambodia

Assisting land mine victims in Cambodia

While traveling in Cambodia in 2001, I visited a rehabilitation center that was supported by a Belgian relief agency. It was located in the town of Siem Riep. More than ten thousand land mines were planted in Cambodia from the 1970s into the early 1990s. The victims of land mine explosions would come from villages across the country to this center to be fitted for prostheses. After two weeks of instruction in the use of their new limbs, they were able to return home and once again become more useful members of their communities.

"Be kind because everyone you meet is fighting a hard battle."
—*BOB DYLAN*

Each of us can contribute

Some friends are also heroes: Geoffrey Tabin, whom I mention previously, is a hero of mine. So is the late Eli Segal. He served as assistant to the president in the Clinton White House. As founding CEO of Americorps, he built and implemented a program that allowed hundreds of thousands of young people to pay for college by performing community service. He was also founding CEO of the Welfare-to-Work Partnership, which encourages businesses to hire people to enable them to end their dependence on welfare.

For many years I found the accomplishments of these friends intimidating. Eventually I realized that each of us has different gifts and capacities. Even though I could not affect the lives of thousands, I could have a positive effect on one person at a time.

Eli Segal

"The greatest crime is to do nothing because we feel we can only do a little."
—ELIE WIESEL

"Use what talents you possess; the woods would be very silent if no birds sang except those that sang best."
—HENRY VAN DYKE

This story helps me to stay grounded when I think that my contribution may be small. After a storm, many starfish were washed onto the shore of a Pacific island. The tide receded and, if the starfish did not return to the ocean, they would not survive. One man walked along the beach and threw several back into the water. An observer said, "Why are you throwing them back? There are so many of them, it won't make any difference." After the man had tossed another starfish into the ocean, he said, "Made a difference to that one."

Hamoa Beach. Maui, Hawaii

Having a mission

According to Maslow, all of the self-actualized people he studied have a mission, or calling—a special duty enlisting their energies in a cause that contributes to the greater good. Their passionate commitment to the work is fulfilling in its own right. Though other paths certainly lead to an enriching life, all of the self-actualized people Maslow observed felt that they were making a difference in the world.

"We cannot all do great things, but we can all do little things with great love."
—MOTHER THERESA

Making our work more meaningful

A recurring theme in this book is that we can create and shape our own realities. Authentic power comes not from what you are doing, but how you are doing it. Although some occupations might appear more significant than others, there are ways to make any type of work feel more meaningful.

An illustration: Two bricklayers in fourteenth-century France were working on the side of the road. When a traveler stopped to inquire what they were doing, one replied, "I am working with bricks." The other proudly stated, "I am building a cathedral!"

Each of us has a certain skill set. Author Gary Zukav elaborates upon this idea in *Soul Stories*, "Some people have hunches, others ideas, some hear music, others see pictures, some hear words. You can find your way by paying attention to what is inside you."

Fishermen. Lake Pátzcuaro, Mexico

Roanji. Kyoto, Japan

"Let the beauty we love be what we do. There are
hundreds of ways to kneel and kiss the ground."
—RUMI

Struggling to make the work meaningful

It can be challenging to discover your individual aptitudes and abilities, much less find a career to match them. This process certainly has been difficult for me. Every job entails an element of drudgery and frustration; the challenge is to make it as enjoyable and meaningful as possible. I did not rise to this task well in medical school.

In 1964 I enrolled at the University of Texas Southwestern Medical School in Dallas. Instantly, I was overwhelmed by medical science classes. Previously, as an undergraduate at Brandeis University, I had developed interests in art, music, and philosophy and had considered several career options, including being an architect, drama critic, and college professor. While in medical school, I naively expected to be able to pursue these interests. However, during the first two years of medical school that was impossible, because every hour of the day was taken up by anatomy, physiology, and microbiology. While many medical school colleagues felt certain, even at a young age, that they would attend medical school, I felt out of place, as though I was in an alien environment, like a fish out of water. I was frightened that I would not survive the medical school grind.

In fact, at the time, I was studying fascinating material and was surrounded by some of the best and brightest people in medicine. I could not yet recognize what a privilege it all was. Looking back, my early medical school experience was laced with frustration because I was not skilled at finding meaning in my work.

Understanding strengths and limitations

It is important to have an accurate understanding of our individual potentials and limitations. From this springs realistic expectations and the presence of mind to adjust them when situations do not turn out as anticipated.

During my psychiatry rotation in medical school, my expectations were once again unrealistic. I enjoyed interacting with patients and felt as if I truly was connecting with them. Unfortunately, behavior patterns do not alter dramatically overnight. Despite several therapy sessions, what I had thought were my brilliant insights did not always result in significant life changes in my patients. I found myself frustrated by the lack of immediate, tangible results. My expectations did not match reality.

Eventually, I realized that psychiatric treatment was typically a long process and that I did not have the patience to wait for the anticipated outcomes. Consequently, I turned to orthopedic surgery, primarily because an immediate tangible result was the rule rather than the exception. A wrist was broken and I could set it; a joint became worn out and I could replace it. Furthermore, I could continue to utilize my interest in people and their behavior. I became more aware of my false expectations and limitations, and was therefore able to make a better-informed career decision.

Making each encounter better

Over time, I have improved my ability to make my work meaningful. I love being a physician, especially treating patients from diverse backgrounds, caring for them in the office, and facing the challenges of the operating room. Of course, for other physicians many other options are available. For example, clinical or laboratory research may be more appealing.

Every patient encounter becomes more valuable when I learn about their background and interests, and share related personal stories. Regardless of a patient's medical problem, each has a uniquely interesting personal history.

Different approaches work for different people. Responding to each patient's different needs and concerns—especially those left unarticulated—can be a challenge.

A few years ago, an elderly woman was wheeled into the operating room by two orderlies. Before she was transferred to the operating table, she stopped us in the midst of our preparations, making an astonishing pronouncement, "I have one request: before we go any further, I want all of you to accept Jesus as your personal savior." There were two orderlies, an anesthesiologist and his assistant, a scrub nurse, circulating nurse, assistant surgeon, and myself. Seeing our shock and reluctance she prodded the orderly beside her, "You, young man, can be the first." "Well, ma'am," he politely ventured, "I'm afraid I can't, because I'm a Black Muslim." I noticed that the patient was becoming increasingly agitated, so I suggested that we all gather around the bed, hold hands and say a prayer for her. We prayed silently for two minutes with our eyes closed. I then said, "Amen." When we opened our eyes to look at her, she took a deep breath, patted her heart, and said, "Ohhh, I feel so much better now—very peaceful." She seemed to be reassured, for which I felt a deep sense of gratitude. By taking a different approach, a difficult situation became a positive one.

Kuna Indian. Panama

On teaching

*"My joy in learning is partly that it enables
me to teach."*
— SENECA

I also love teaching and consider it a noble profession.
For me, it is an honor to have trained resident physicians
from a wide variety of backgrounds: India, Pakistan,
Iraq, Iran, the Philippines, Korea, Ghana, Haiti, Cuba,
Canada, Bosnia, Egypt, Gaza, Israel, Panama, Puerto
Rico, Argentina, Colombia, and the United States. They
have included Muslims, Sikhs, Hindus, Copts, Orthodox
Jews, Catholics, and evangelical Christians.

The thought that I have nurtured, taught, and, hopefully,
positively influenced such a varied group of young
physicians gives me great joy. Teaching is a challenge.
I try to push myself to a higher standard by rethinking
what I consider to be true in the face of students who
may be free of my assumptions and biases.

There are several principles I try to get across to resident
physicians. No matter what problem the patient arrives
with, they should leave feeling better, and there are many
ways to make this happen. First, it is essential to be
fully present. If one is thinking about tomorrow's golf
game during the examination, any patient will feel the
lack of attention. Second, words are important, as is
body language. A substantial part of communication
is nonverbal, so the manner in which a diagnosis is
communicated is sometimes more important than the
diagnosis itself. Third, I try to communicate the elegance
of the science when discussing principles of anatomy,
physiology, and bioengineering. Last, in addition to
being scientists, physicians are citizens of the world.
Cross-cultural communication is a critical skill.
Therefore I assign topics for the residents to discuss,
such as the history, culture, and politics of a patient's
country. The goal is to make future encounters
with patients from that region more meaningful, for
both the patient and doctor.

*"Better to know what sort of person has the disease
than to know what disease the patient has."*
— WILLIAM OSLER, M.D.

I try my best to create an indelible learning experience.
Teaching is an honor. Receiving a best teacher award
from the Rush Medical School and Hospital Center was
one of my proudest moments.

Keel-billed toucan. Honduras

"I'd love to kiss you but I just washed my hair."
—BETTE DAVIS, IN THE MOVIE
'THE CABIN IN THE COTTON.' SCREENPLAY
BY PAUL GREEN.

6.

Humor and Celebration

Abraham Maslow observed that the self-actualized have a great capacity for laughter, playfulness, love, and joy. They have an optimistic attitude toward everyday life. As Maslow writes, "Self-actualized people enjoy life in general and practically all its aspects, while most other people enjoy only stray moments of triumph." Fortunately, each of us is capable of increasing our capacity for joy.

Savoring life's joys

Although diverse cultures may define pleasurable experiences differently, childlike joy appears to be universal. My family and I experienced a memorable example of this on a recent visit to Israel. We traveled to the Dead Sea, famed for its mud, which has been used for thousands of years to provide relief for skin disorders such as psoriasis and eczema. The mud is marketed worldwide.

Korean woman. Dead Sea, Israel

Soon after we arrived there, a busload of Korean women on a Bible study mission appeared. Initially they gave the impression of being a most orderly group, but when they proceeded to rub Dead Sea mud all over their bodies, these seemingly reserved women were suddenly giggling and laughing like five-year-olds. My family, similarly covered in mud, wordlessly exchanged hilarious glances with these women and each other, and then fell into tears-rolling-down-your face, holding-your-sides, uncontrollable laughter.

Celebrating with friends

Elie Wiesel, in *Against Silence*, writes, "Popular belief has it that true friendship can be ascertained only in time of need. Not so; in happiness you will recognize your true friends. They will not be envious. You will usually find friends to feel sorry for you but rare are those who feel happy simply because you are happy."

"Let your friend's fortune be as dear to you as your own."
—*AMOS OZ*

Among life's great pleasures is celebrating with friends and, when rejoicing with them, I often think of Wiesel's words. Remembering the positive energy that I have felt from friends on my own happy occasions, I always attempt to fully participate in the joy of their special events. We should exercise our capacity for celebration.

"There are halls in the heavens above that open only to song."
—*THE ZOHAR*

Michael Lewis and daughter Melanie. Dead Sea, Israel

Maintaining a sense of humor

Maslow found that humor in self-actualized people is not hostile and does not laugh at someone else's inferiority. Instead, it pokes fun with a positive slant. David and Daniel Hayes are a father-and-son team who sailed around the world together in a twenty-five-foot boat, which they built together. They were in each other's company for twenty-four hours a day, often in difficult circumstances. This required the establishment of basic ground rules. In their book, *My Old Man and the Sea*, they state, "We remember our #1 rule, the big rule, or B. R. If you're going to laugh about something in six months or a year, you might as well start laughing now."

"Strange that of all the countless folk who have lived on this planet, not one is known in history or legend as having died of laughter."
—MAX BEERBOHM

Michael Lewis. Wichita Falls, Texas, 1973

Handling humility with humor

On many occasions I have been shown the folly of taking myself too seriously. After I finished my orthopedic residency in 1973, I spent two years in the United States Air Force. Before being sent off to our respective bases, all newly minted medical officers were given uniforms and taught to salute and march during basic training at Sheppard Air Force Base in Wichita Falls, Texas.

Initially we thought the idea of marching rather silly, especially since we would be working full time as physicians. In spite of this, we soon found that we rather enjoyed this group activity, and we began to see the point of establishing *esprit de corps*. Therefore, we were especially proud when our sergeant and group leader said, after we finished parading, that the general in charge of our base had just observed us and was pleased. The sergeant paused just long enough to get our attention, then pronounced with a perfectly dead-pan expression, "Pleased that all of you will be going to other bases."

I was again reminded not to take myself too seriously after I was an orthopedic consultant to the Chicago Bulls basketball team. In the world of sports, it was a high-profile, dream-come-true job. To some people, my wit, charm, and IQ noticeably improved during that time. I was pleased with my newly acquired personality upgrade. Unfortunately, when my tour as a team physician ended, my personality appeared to lose its luster and rapidly returned to its pedestrian, pre-Bulls level.

Ed Paschke, the well-known Chicago artist, wrote an essay about himself titled "Yang and Yin at Comiskey Park." In 1990, the Art Institute of Chicago presented a retrospective of his work—quite a feat for a local, living artist. Soon after the exhibit opened, Paschke was at a Chicago White Sox baseball game at the old Comiskey Park, when a hot dog vendor recognized and con-gratulated him on the show. Ed was feeling quite full of himself, thinking perhaps he really was becoming famous, when suddenly pigeon droppings from the rafters landed on his head. Paschke wrote that this quickly restored the proper balance between yang and yin and his rightful place in the universe.

Elton Brand and Michael Lewis during a Bulls game

Photograph courtesy Todd Buchanan

Bill Veeck

Fun at the old ball park

Because I have been an orthopedic consultant for professional sports teams, I am often asked who is the most memorable person I have met in the world of sports. Although I have had contact with some larger-than-life names—Michael Jordan, Dennis Rodman, Phil Jackson, Harry Carey, Jimmy Piersall, Goose Gossage, Wilbur Wood—without hesitation, my answer is Bill Veeck.

I was most fortunate to spend time with Veeck when he was the owner of the Chicago White Sox. He was filled with creative energy and was always thinking of ways to bring more fun and excitement to the game. He once showed me files of index cards on which he wrote ideas as they popped into his head. He had invented such traditions as the exploding scoreboard, having players take curtain calls after they hit a home run, and the singing of "Take Me Out to the Ballgame" during the seventh-inning stretch.

Veeck was a brilliant promoter. His book, *Veeck as in Wreck*, was a best seller. He established Fan Appreciation Night. On one occasion, he gave away orchids to all the female fans, and on another, a sweltering midsummer night, he presented a two-hundred-pound block of ice to one lucky fan. He is well remembered for sending 3-foot, 6 1/2-inch Eddie Gaedel to the plate in 1951. Gaedel walked on four pitches.

Bill Veeck was much more than just a clever promoter. He also achieved tangible results. In 1948, while owner of the Cleveland Indians, his team won a World Series, and in 1959 his Chicago White Sox won the American League pennant.

Veeck retained his sense of playfulness even in challenging times. He told me this story: the St. Louis Browns had the lowest attendance in the league. In the box office, Veeck thought it not unusual to pick up the telephone. Once, a fan called and asked what time Saturday's game was going to start. Bill replied, "How many in your party?" The man answered, "Six." Bill's response was, "What time would be convenient for you?"

Gentoo Penguins. South Georgia Island

"Those who danced were thought to be quite insane by those who could not hear the music."
—*ANGELA MONET*

"*Angels can fly because they take
themselves lightly.*"
—G. K. CHESTERTON

Sandhill cranes. Platte River, Nebraska

Developing an optimistic attitude

Self-actualized people have an optimistic attitude. Fortunately, each of us can increase our capacity for optimism. One way to accomplish this is to recognize the importance of expressing gratitude. In *The How of Happiness*, Sonja Lyubomirsky establishes that keeping a gratitude journal will increase one's satisfaction with life. She suggests a weekly entry, recording three to five things for which you are thankful.

It appears that people have understood the importance of gratitude for centuries. An ancient Hebrew expression and the title to a popular song sung at the Passover seder, *dayenu* means "It is enough for us," or "We would have been satisfied." It acknowledges the gifts we have received. It reminds us to be grateful for the present moment and to work with what we have been given.

"I'm grateful that I can be grateful."
—*BEATRICE LEWIS*

It may seem like a simple idea, but thoughts can be self-fulfilling. Social science has observed that optimistic people are more likely to obtain the results they are seeking. For example, if you are confident that you will be able to achieve a goal, you will invest more effort to reach it. Brendan Gill, who wrote *Here at the New Yorker*, delightfully describes his optimistic state. "I leap out of bed in the morning with the disposition that something perfectly wonderful is going to happen that day."

Cultivating compassion

Richard Davidson, a neuroscientist at the University of Wisconsin, has a special interest in neuroplasticity, which is the capacity of the brain to develop and change throughout life. He has performed studies measuring the ability to generate emotional compassion by asking his subjects to meditate on unconditional loving-kindness and compassion. He measured the results using sophisticated tools, including qualitative electrophysiology and functional magnetic resonance imaging.

Davidson compared Tibetan Buddhists experienced in meditation with a control group of college students inexperienced in meditation. One study demonstrated that the Tibetans produced gamma waves that were thirty times as strong as the students' results. Imagine! Just thinking about an emotion can produce changes in brain electrical impulses and chemistry. Admittedly, it is a leap from thinking about compassion to acting compassionately. However, this study suggests that happiness and compassion potentially are skills that can be developed and exercised, like playing a musical instrument.

I have asked the following of numerous medical educators: can compassion be taught? Davidson's research begins to address this subject. Imagine if our educational system devoted more time to researching and teaching techniques that could increase compassion!

In 1972, in the mountain kingdom of Bhutan, King Jigme Wangchuck coined the term "Gross National Happiness" (GNH). We appear to be at the beginning of an era when we can learn how to increase our GNH. Perhaps the message that I received in 1969 in San Francisco was correct after all: this is the Age of Aquarius, and we are, indeed, entering a time of love, light, and humanity.

"The good new days are today and better days are coming tomorrow. Our greatest songs are still unsung."
—HUBERT HUMPHREY

Buddhist Monk. Siem Riep, Cambodia

Children. Washington, Louisiana

7.

Kinship

Abraham Maslow writes that the self-actualized have a great capacity for friendship. They possess a deep feeling of identification with, and sympathy and affection for, all living things. Since they are secure in themselves and cultivate their own talents and identity, they have the power to love freely and easily.

The ancient Greeks described several types of love. They included *philia*, meaning friendship; *agape*, a divine love or brotherly love for all humanity; and *eros*, an erotic or sexual love. Philia and agape are discussed in this chapter. Eros is discussed in the next chapter.

Aristotle described several types of friendship, including friendships of reciprocal concern, friendships of pleasure (those that share activities or hobbies), and utilitarian friendships, characterized by many business relationships. Abraham Maslow added democratic friendships, defined as the ability to relate well to people of varied backgrounds.

Young monks. Punakha, Bhutan

The value of friendship

Socrates wrote about how important friendship was to him. "All people have their fancies; some desire horses, and others dogs, and some are fond of gold, and others of honour. But I have a passion for friends. I should greatly prefer a real friend to all the gold of Darius."

"All love that has not friendship for its base, is like a mansion built upon sand."
—ELLA WHEELER WILCOX

In *Man's Search for Meaning,* a memoir portraying life in the Nazi death camps, Viktor E. Frankl reflects on methods of survival, including thinking only of oneself. According to Frankl, that was the wrong strategy. A survivor himself, he saw that those who thought of others—a family member or comrade for whom he or she cared—had a better chance of survival.

More than fifty years ago I was given a book of essays written by American philosopher Ralph Waldo Emerson. It includes a treatise on friendship, which I have re-read many times. Emerson emphasizes that friends mirror our values, giving us keen insight into our place in the world. Friends are extensions of ourselves, even part of our essence. He stirringly notes, "The ancients exchanged their names with their friends, signifying that in their friend they loved their own soul."

The short list

For Aristotle, friendship's highest form is one of reciprocal concern between two people. Consider the people you can count on in any situation; I call this the short list. Because we have a limited amount of time and emotional energy, there are only so many people with whom we can feel deeply connected. Many sociologists and anthropologists have concluded that if a clan, tribe, or organization is composed of more than 150 people, cohesiveness is lost. It is sobering to think that although I may have touched the lives of thousands—in some small way—only a few have been significantly affected. The short list is just that: short.

"Go through your phone book, call people and ask them to drive you to the airport. The ones who will drive you are your true friends. The rest aren't bad people, they are just acquaintances."
—JAY LENO

When I was younger, I thought it inevitable that as I aged and met more people, my number of close friends would naturally grow. To my surprise, this has not happened as I predicted. However, established relationships have continued to deepen. Shared history seems to be more important than I had anticipated. For a new friendship to develop, a commitment of time and energy is required. This becomes more difficult because, as we become older, our lives become more consumed by personal and professional commitments.

When we are younger, some of us have the luxury of sharing a great variety of circumstances with our friends. For example, as roommates in college, one sees all facets of a person, such as their actions in the classroom and on the athletic field, as well as how they handle a love affair gone awry.

How can we increase our prospects for friendship? Participating in a variety of activities together can help develop rapport. Aristotle labeled these friendships of pleasure. Here is a personal example: I am a member of a book club consisting of eleven men that has been in existence for more than forty years. With several members, what began as a shared interest in books has evolved into deeper personal relationships.

Ringtailed lemurs. Madagascar

Two friends. Todi, Umbria, Italy

"A friend is a person with whom I may be sincere.
Before him, I may think aloud."
—RALPH WALDO EMERSON

Utilitarian friendships

Aristotle named another category of friendship *utilitarian*, which he defines as a relationship that is mutually useful. This term characterizes many types of business relationships. I have been slow to appreciate the distinctions between different types of friendships. For example, having spent days—even years—making life and death decisions together with other physicians, I imagined that close friendships would naturally occur. I have not found that this is the case. Although I do have close friendships with some of my professional colleagues, most seem to correspond to the utilitarian category.

Dan Ariely, a professor of behavioral economics at Duke University, gives one explanation in *Predictably Irrational*. His book is about how people live simultaneously in two worlds. One is the business world of market norms: wages, prices, and cost-benefit analyses. The other is of social norms: recreation, friendships, and family. I recognize that multiple types of relationships are necessary. However, it appears to me that market norms have dominated our society, and too often we define one another by how we earn a living. We can change the equation by treating each other more holistically in the work environment. As Ariely points out, "Life with fewer market norms and more social norms would be more satisfying, creative, fulfilling, and fun."

It was exhilarating to be a part of the Chicago Bulls basketball team's incredible championship ride in the 1990s. I have often thought the experience similar to what it might have been like traveling with the Beatles in the 1960s. However, it was disappointing to me that, in spite of sharing this unique experience, close relationships that developed at the time proved transient. Ex-players, trainers, and managers have since acknowledged to me that friendships in professional sports are frequently temporary.

It has taken me many years to appreciate that there are many types of friendship and that sometimes they overlap.

Democratic friendships

According to Maslow, the self-actualized feel kinship and connection as if all people were members of a single family. Maslow refers to this as having democratic friendships, which are characterized by being able to relate well to people of different ages, as well as varied intellectual, social, and ethnic backgrounds.

Bill Veeck could be a poster child for democratic friendships, and he is a real role model for me in this area. As previously mentioned, I got to know him well when he was the owner of the Chicago White Sox in the mid-seventies, while I was associated with the team.

Bill had a remarkable ability to relate to a broad range of people on many levels. For example, he was very literate. An author himself, he read several books a week. Because his amputated leg required treatment in a bath for an hour each morning, he used the time to read novels. He was therefore very comfortable discussing literature with the journalists covering the team.

He had served as a medic during the Korean War, and had undergone several surgeries himself. Thus, he knew medical lingo and was comfortable around doctors and other medical personnel. The team's players, including pitching star Wilbur Wood, had great respect and admiration for Veeck, and felt comfortable discussing both professional and personal issues with him. In addition, because he was a true devotee of the game of baseball, he identified with his paying customers, the Chicago White Sox fans.

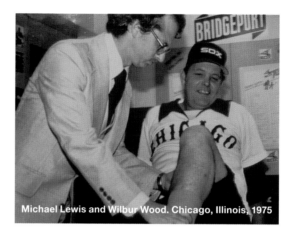

Michael Lewis and Wilbur Wood. Chicago, Illinois, 1975

I have often thought that he embodied the true meaning of sophistication: comfortable with himself, he made those around him more comfortable, no matter the person or the setting. Bill just loved being with people and knew that everyone had an interesting story to tell. He loved to listen and to learn from everyone.

William Gladstone and Benjamin Disraeli were two famous British prime ministers of the nineteenth century. It was said that after you dined with Gladstone, you left thinking that he was one of the most intelligent and interesting men you had ever met. After you had dinner with Disraeli, you left thinking that *you* were a smart and interesting person. Disraeli, like Bill Veeck, knew how to make others feel appreciated and important.

"You can make more friends in two months by becoming really interested in other people, than you can in two years by trying to get other people interested in you."
—DALE CARNEGIE

Spirituality

Maslow used the word *spiritual* to characterize the self-actualized. Agape is love with a spiritual connotation. It can be defined in different ways, including God's love for humanity, and man's love for God. For others it is an expression of love and kinship, through feelings of thoughtfulness, generosity, and kindness toward their fellow man; a desire to make the world a better place; and a commitment to creating a loving environment in which all can thrive.

"The essence of true religious teaching is that one should serve and befriend all."
—MAHATMA GANDHI

Mircea Eliade, a professor of religion at the University of Chicago, observes in *The Sacred and the Profane*, that there is a universal human characteristic: the perception that the world has a sacred quality to it.

Spirituality is commonly defined as a search for the sacred without necessarily including a belief in God. Shared by both religion and spirituality is the deep sense of interconnectedness with the world. Both may generate within us a sense of wonder at the grandeur and mystery of life, and both can guide us to focus on problems outside of ourselves. Both religion and spirituality can lead to an understanding of the sanctity of places and of time and help us perceive our family and friends as blessings. Maslow described the self-actualized as strongly ethical with definite moral standards. Not all of them, however, participate in an organized religion.

"Every deed counts and every word has power. We should build our life as if it were a work of art."
—ABRAHAM JOSHUA HESCHEL

Respecting other forms of worship

The importance of respecting one another's form of worship has been expressed by countless religious and spiritual leaders. Professors of psychology Kenneth I. Pargament and Annette Mahoney have articulated this idea particularly well in their lectures. "We have to be sensitive to the diverse ways people experience and express their spirituality. In the search for the sacred, people take many different pathways toward many different destinations. We must respect the full range of worldviews, practices and communities that people form in their spiritual journeys." It is important to respect others for what they are, and not to disrespect them for what they are not.

One of the principal challenges in the world today is finding the balance between respecting the spiritual journeys of others while protecting ourselves from religious extremists. Respect means to recognize and honor my freedom as well as yours.

"Do not say 'I follow the one true path of the Spirit,' but rather, 'I have found the Spirit walking on my path,' for the Spirit walks on all paths."
—KHALIL GIBRAN

Namaste, originally a Sanskrit word, is now used as a greeting in many cultures around the world. It has a rich spiritual connotation. It conveys, in essence, that the divinity within me perceives the divinity within you, and all that is best and highest in me salutes all that is best and highest in you. What an ideal approach for connecting with another person!

"Let us deal kindly with one another. We are all pilgrims on the same road which leads to the same end."
—HYMAN JUDAH SCHACHTEL

Tibetan prayer flags. Santa Fe, New Mexico

Appreciating the world around us

Maslow describes the self-actualized as having love and sympathy for all humanity, including not only our children and our children's children, but also many future generations. This idea is well expressed in a recent television interview with Oren Lyons, the Onondago Indian tribe faithkeeper. "In our way of life, with every decision we make, we always keep in mind the seventh generation to come. It is our job to see that the generations still unborn have a world no worse than ours, and hopefully better. When we walk upon Mother Earth we always plant our feet carefully because we know the faces of our future generations are looking up at us from beneath the ground. We never forget them."

The Onondago Indians are keenly aware of the interconnection between people, fauna, and flora of the Earth. They understand the importance of maintaining equilibrium, and appreciating the patterns of natural cycles. Payson R. Stevens speaks of these interlocking connections in *Embracing Earth: New Views of Our Changing Planet*. "Patterns and structure. Everywhere we look we see them. Cycles and rhythms. Pulses and flows. Changes in magnetic fields. Continental plates moving. Water cycles. Seasons changing. Life and death. Process and connection. Nature flows through webs of structure and shifting time: from ocean to cloud to rain to river to ocean. Natural rhythms."

All living things on this planet have carved out specific niches for themselves. The oilbird illustrates this point. Found in neotropical forests, these birds live in caves, and feed on the fruit of the oil palm and tropical laurels. They search for fruit in a flock, because the more eyes searching for food, the better the chance of finding it. When fruit is ripe, there is plenty for all. The birds search for fruit at night because they are one of the few birds known to navigate by echolocation, which enables them to find their way in low light or in the dark. But why do they live in a cave? The answer is the absence of competition and of predators. On a diet with so much fruit and little protein, the young are slow to develop. If the birds nested anywhere in the rainforest other than a cave, they would be especially vulnerable to predators, including snakes, monkeys, and other birds. It is astonishing to think that each living creature, like the oilbird, occupies a unique position in the delicate balance of nature.

"We are all notes in the same grand symphony."
—BILL WITTLIFF

Polar bears, Churchill, Manitoba, Canada

Recently I was in Manitoba, Canada. I was there to witness the gathering of polar bears, which takes place in the month of November on a peninsula jutting into Hudson Bay near the town of Churchill. They had been on the mainland since the spring, and now they were waiting for sufficient ice to form in order to live on the Arctic ice floes and feed on seals. Young mothers were snuggling and napping together with their cubs. Meanwhile, the young males spent much of the day fighting. They would rise up on their two hind legs and spar. This was just for practice. In a few weeks, when they would be hunting on the ice floes, the fighting between each other over territory and shortage of food could become ferocious, resulting in serious injury or even death.

Global warming is the most significant threat to the polar bear, because the melting of ice in the Arctic Ocean results in less territory from which they can hunt for food. Since 1980, female polar bears in that area have lost 20 percent of their weight on average, and the polar bear population has declined by more than 20 percent.

Helping to protect the future

The decline of the polar bear population is one indication, on a long list, that radical changes are occurring around the globe. Our planet simply cannot sustain the present rate of destruction of the environment.

"I did not find the world desolate when I entered it. As my fathers planted for me before I was born, I now plant for those who will come after me."
—THE TALMUD

Our actions are shaping the kind of world we will be leaving for future generations. What can we do to help secure our planet for them? We can start by better understanding the concept of our ecological footprint. This tool weighs our lifestyle and consumption against nature's ability to replace this expenditure. The choices we make in our homes, the food we eat, and what we buy and throw away all influence our footprint.

"Science and religion are two of the most potent forces on Earth, and they should come together to save the creation."
—E. O. WILSON

Dead Lake, Namib-Naukluft National Park, Namibia

Calving glacier. Alaska

Excuses for not acting are readily available: the task is overwhelming and there is so little that one can do. Rather than dwell on those negatives, we can, like the story of the man who returned starfish to the ocean, take it one step at a time.

We can think of Maslow's notion of kinship in a broader way that includes all living things. We can continually question how our actions will affect future generations. To improve the likelihood of a viable planet for my grandson, I intend to make better choices.

"I expect to pass through this world but once. Any good thing therefore that I can do, or any kindness that I can show to any fellow creature, let me do it now for I shall not pass this way again."
—STEPHEN GRELLET

8.

Loving and Being Loved

While acknowledging that love is difficult to quantify scientifically, Abraham Maslow in his book, *Motivation and Personality*, allocates as much space to the subject of love in the self-actualized as he does in describing all their other characteristics combined. He frequently emphasized that important questions should be addressed even if they are difficult to define. Attempting to understand the nature of love fits into this category.

In this chapter, *eros*, or sexual love is discussed along with other aspects of love. For some people, love is simply sexual. Maslow finds this definition too restricted. He describes the self-actualized as experiencing love that seeks no cause beyond enjoyment, contemplation, and the appreciation of the significant other. There is an intense feeling of tenderness, affection, growing intimacy, and honesty. There is great pleasure in the journey itself, which is filled with joy, laughter, and affirmation of the loved one.

Defining love

Is love simply sexual—a chemical reaction, a clever device by Mother Nature to ensure the continuation of the species? Arthur Schopenhauer argued for the case. The nineteenth-century German philosopher's book, *The World as Will and Representation*, foreshadowed Sigmund Freud. "All love, however ethereally it may bear itself, is rooted in the sexual impulse alone, nay, it absolutely is only a more definitely determined, specialized, and indeed, in the strictest sense, individualized sexual impulse."

A century later, Sigmund Freud wrote in *Three Essays on the Theory of Sexuality*, "The nucleus of what we mean by love naturally consists in sexual love with sexual union as its aim. The feelings of sympathy, friendship, trust and so forth which we expend in life are genetically connected with sexuality and have developed out of purely sexual desires, however pure and non-sensual they may appear."

Psychologist Robert J. Sternberg expanded the definition of love in *A Triangular Theory of Love*. According to his theory, love has three components: passion, intimacy, and commitment. Each relationship has a different balance of these elements, which can be independent of one other.

Joy in the relationship

"My mouth tastes sweet with your name on it."
—*RUMI*

Rumi was a thirteenth-century Sufi mystic and poet from the Persian Empire. Even though he speaks to us from a different time, he is one of the most popular poets in the United States today.

Many of Rumi's most potent expressions of love are gathered in *Rumi: The Path of Love* by Manuela Dunn Mascetti. Rumi captures the day-to-day joys of sharing life together with a significant other. "The enchantment of lovers is nourished by intimacy, and it is measured in the small moments of life. Cherish these sweet moments you share, sitting quietly, feeling the water of life flowing, watching the garden's beauty and listening to the birds singing. It is the cup of tea you drink together, the holding each other before falling asleep, in the finding yourselves intertwined when you awake. It is always and everywhere, but secretly. Intimacy is the lubricant of the heart—with it, everything is rendered fluid and sweet, like honey."

Such joy is echoed by Pablo Neruda, the Chilean writer who won the Nobel Prize in literature in 1971. In *100 Love Sonnets*, he writes, "Let's go, get up – pin back your hair – take off and land, run and sing with the air and me."

To paraphrase Maslow, if you are not struck dumb by your significant other once in a while, you are missing something—you are being blind to something which is there.

"I love you. On your lips I kiss happiness itself."
—*PABLO NERUDA*

Affirmation of the loved one

A self-actualized person affirms the other's individuality and loves the other person as they are. At the same time, he or she derives great pleasure from watching the loved one grow and thrive.

"Love is that condition in which the happiness of another person is essential to your own."
—*ROBERT HEINLEIN*

Trumpet flowers. Kauai, Hawaii, USA

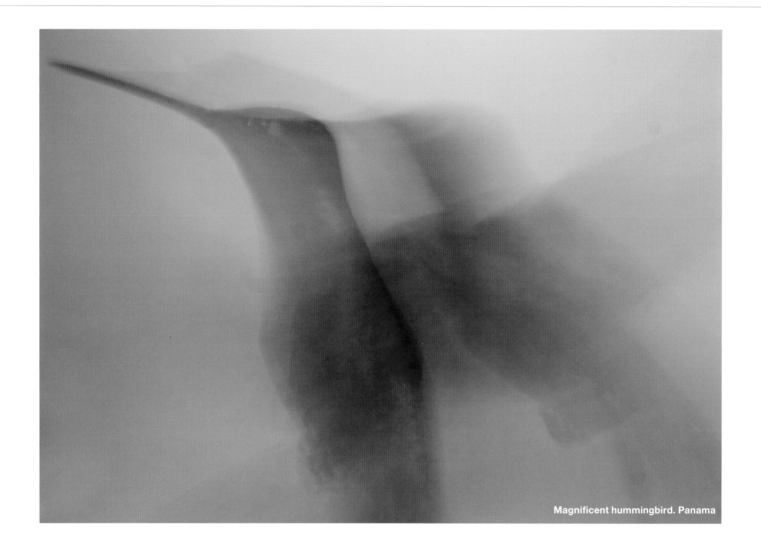

Magnificent hummingbird. Panama

"The beginning of love is to let those we love be perfectly themselves, and not to twist them to fit our own image. Otherwise, we love only a reflection of ourselves we find in them."
—THOMAS MERTON

There is a delicate balance between offering unconditional love and encouraging a loved one to reach his or her highest potential. When we become more comfortable with ourselves we are more likely to be able to find this happy medium.

I come from the most loving, demonstrative family I know. My parents set that tone. Although my father died in 1999, my mother, Beatrice Lewis, continues to be the model par excellence for devotion to family. Now in her ninth decade, she amazes everyone with her energy, generosity, passion, and insight. She is a tough act to follow, but an inspiring example. I feel such gratitude for the affirmation of my family—it makes it easy to want to be nurturing to others. Nonetheless, nurturing is a challenge, especially with one's own children.

"Unconditional love is loving your kids for who they are, not for what they do. It is not something you will achieve every minute of the day. But it is the thought we must hold in our hearts everyday."
—STEPHANIE MARSTON

According to Maslow, being autonomous and having a full life outside of their relationship enables two people to enrich each other with their separate gifts. At the same time, the best relationships share many common interests. Since self-actualized people are so comfortable with themselves, they are less demanding in their relationships and are easily able to give partners their own space.

Wedding. Santa Clara del Cobre, Mexico

Expressing love

In his book *Tuesdays with Morrie*, Mitch Albom quotes his friend Morrie Schwartz, who said, "The most important thing in life is to learn how to give out love and to let it come in. Love is the only rational act."

In the pages of *The Seven Principles of Making Marriage Work*, John Gottman, professor emeritus of psychology at the University of Washington, discusses a formula that I think about every day: the five-to-one ratio. After thousands of videotaped sessions of volunteer couples, a study revealed a noteworthy conclusion about successful relationships: there is an ongoing ratio of five positive interactions for every one negative interaction. This ratio takes into account any negative events, both within the relationship and outside of it. The five-to-one ratio held for the smallest as well as the grandest gestures. Little things matter. Small courtesies and affectionate gestures are important and should take place every day. If the proportion of positive to negative communications becomes higher than five to one, the relationship has a much better chance for success.

Bald eagles. Ketchikan, Alaska

"A good marriage is that in which each appoints the other guardian of his solitude."
—*RAINER MARIA RILKE*

Spoonbills. High Island, Texas

"*Experience shows us that love does not consist in gazing at each other but in looking together in the same direction.*"
—ANTOINE DE SAINT-EXUPERY

Love is a choice one makes moment by moment. A loving environment does not just happen. It requires a conscious effort. Every relationship is unique, and compromise is important. At the least, one must be able to sympathize with the significant other's point of view.

"Love doesn't just sit there like a stone; it has to be made like bread, remade all the time, made new."
—URSULA K. LEGUIN

Edward Lear penned the poem, *The Owl and the Pussycat,* in which he invented the nonsense word *runcible,* as in runcible spoon. By describing a simple, everyday utensil in a magical way, Lear captures the daily commonplace pleasures of a loving relationship.

"The owl and the pussycat went to sea in a beautiful pea green boat.
They took some honey and plenty of money wrapped up in a five pound note….
They dined on mince and slices of quince which they ate with a runcible spoon.
And hand and hand on the edge of the sand, they danced by the light of the moon.
They danced by the light of the moon."

In *100 Love Sonnets,* Pablo Neruda emphasizes the desire to experience everything about the significant other. "I want to eat the sunbeam flaring in your lovely body… I want to eat the fleeting shade of your lashes."

Sappho, one of the first known female poets, lived in ancient Greece in the seventh century B.C.E. She potently expressed the erotic element in love. "When I look at you a moment I can speak no more, and at once a delicate flame courses beneath my skin, and a wet sweat bathes me, and a trembling seizes me all over."

Tango dancers. Buenos Aires, Argentina

Woman with cigar. Havana, Cuba

Love and laughter

"Among those people who I like or admire, I can find no common denominator, but among those I love I can—all of them make me laugh."
—W. H. AUDEN

For the self-actualized, love with a significant other is often cheerful and humorous.

"Love is an exploding cigar we willingly smoke."
—LYNDA BARRY

Joanne Woodward was married to the late Paul Newman, considered to have been one of the sexiest men of his generation. Knowing this, Woodward's oft-quoted remark might surprise you. "Sexiness wears thin after awhile and beauty fades, but to be married to a man who makes you laugh every day, ah, now that's a real treat."

"It's not the men in my life that counts. It's the life in my men."
—MAE WEST

Listening with an open heart

Over time, intimacy and honesty grow for the self-actualized, and the feeling of freedom with a significant other develops. It is exhilarating to be psychologically naked and vulnerable, and yet feel as if you are in a safe haven, deeply understood and accepted.

The self-actualized know how to create a loving, nurturing environment, and how to listen with a clear mind and an open heart. Dinah Craik, a nineteenth-century English novelist and poet, summarized this well in *A Life for a Life*: "Oh the comfort, the inexpressible comfort of feeling safe with a person – having neither to weigh thoughts or measure words, but pouring them all right out, just as they are, chaff and grain together, certain that a faithful hand will take and sift them, keep what is worth keeping, and then with the breath of kindness, blow the rest away."

It is paramount to keep these thoughts in perspective. On the one hand, it is important to feel secure enough in the presence of a significant other to express one's thoughts without inhibition. At the same time, it is important to consider the possible impact of one's words and to listen with an open heart.

All of us have disappointments—frequently and throughout life. We have experiences that are embarrassing or even humiliating. Everyone messes up on occasion. We act in regrettable ways. I find it comforting to be able to confide these things to my significant other. Our relationship has grown because my ability to be open has grown.

"Trouble is part of your life, and if you don't share it, you don't give the person who loves you a chance to love you enough."
—*DINAH SHORE*

Rose bush on wall. Westport, Ireland

*"You are suspended in me beautiful and frozen,
I preserve you, in me you are safe."*
—MARGARET ATWOOD

Long-term relationships

Maslow found that self-actualized love relationships improve and deepen with time. There is intense joy in sharing all aspects of life. Fortunately, this can be true for the rest of us as well.

"A happy relationship is a long conversation that always seems too short."
—ANDRÉ MAUROIS

Toward the end of *War and Peace*, Leo Tolstoy writes about the characters Natasha and Pierre, who had been married for many years. "They began to talk as only a husband and wife can talk, understanding and expressing each other's thoughts in ways contrary to all rules of logic. Natasha suddenly exclaimed, 'What nonsense it is, about honeymoons, and that the greatest happiness is at first. On the contrary, now, after many years, is the best of all.'"

In the final analysis, love remains indefinable and, at the same time, transformative. Once again, Rumi captures love's enchantment. "Love is a secret gateway into a world of mystery, a crossing from one reality to another. Once on the other shore, we perceive in ways that were not possible before, and indeed we become more of what we truly are. Love is like a magic potion that once drunk leads you into the alchemy of complete transformation."

Valerie Dewar Searle Lewis

Even after more than thirty-five years of marriage, the more time I spend with my wife, Valerie Dewar Searle Lewis, the more I appreciate her. I first met her at a United States Air Force base in Lakenheath, England, where I was assigned as an orthopedic surgeon. I was overwhelmed by her sophistication, world travels, and humility. She had been in Ghana with the Voluntary Services Overseas (VSO), the British equivalent of the Peace Corps, and had taught in Argentina and Japan. She had crossed Russia on the trans-Siberian railroad.

I love the idea of viewing my wife in the context of Maslow's characteristics of the self-actualized. She creates her own reality in a most imaginative way. For example, after finishing her tour of duty in the VSO, she was given a ticket for her airfare from Ghana to Britain, but thought that it would be more interesting to return to Britain by hitchhiking across the Sahara desert.

Valerie has great strength of character and is independent in her thinking. She is intensely involved in several causes, including teaching English to adult immigrants, and Human Writes, an organization that supports people on death row. She deeply identifies with her fellow human beings, and is strongly committed to making a better world. She does not wait to be told what a situation requires, but is proactive in a most positive way, always following through on any commitment she makes.

Valerie Dewar Searle Lewis

She has remarkable flexibility, and an exceptional ability to laugh at herself. She has a deep-rooted sense of modesty. Since she is comfortable with herself, she makes everyone around her more comfortable. She knows how to listen with an open heart. She is able, when necessary, to submerge her own interests to the needs of others—a helpful quality considering she has a demanding husband.

Valerie's family and friends adore her, and I have never met anyone who does not have great respect and admiration for her. I cannot imagine a better role model for our children. Each day I learn about passion, intimacy, and commitment from my wife. I strive to be worthy of her.

"And now you're mine. Rest with your dream
in my dream.
We will go together over the waters of time.
No one else will travel through the
shadows with me,
Only you, evergreen, ever sun, ever moon."
—*PABLO NERUDA*

9.

Peak
Experiences

Abraham Maslow coined the term *peak experiences* and wrote extensively about them. He described them as especially joyous moments in life, involving sudden intense feelings of happiness and well-being. These experiences can happen to any of us, even if we are a long way from self-actualization.

What is a peak experience?

According to Abraham Maslow's description, a peak experience happens spontaneously and without warning. It may occur after exposure to great art or music or natural wonders. It may be triggered by seeing a child for the first time. It may take place when participating in an athletic event or sexual act or while meditating. A peak experience is one of the most blissful moments in one's life. It may last from seconds to minutes.

Lake Patzcuaro. Mexico

Maslow explains that during the experience there is a wider sense of awareness, and an absence of one's usual boundaries of time and space. In his words, "We feel one with the world, fused with it, really belonging in it and to it, instead of being outside looking in. These moments are of pure, positive happiness when all doubts, fears, inhibitions, tensions, and weaknesses are left behind. Self-consciousness is lost." A peak experience is a non-evaluating and non-judging state.

Similar experiences were noted at the beginning of the twentieth century by American psychologist and philosopher William James in his book, *The Varieties of Religious Experience.* He reported that many of the great mystics in history had used similar words—not having a sense of time and space, subject and object becoming one—to describe these occurrences. Maslow chose the term *peak* instead of *mystical* because his research showed that the experience could occur in any culture and was not limited to a religious context.

Why peak experiences are important

Why do peak experiences matter? According to Abraham Maslow, people who have had a peak experience describe it as being something extremely important and valuable. It is evidence that joy, ecstasy, and rapture do, in fact, exist. These mystical moments communicate to us a poetic perception of reality, which we would hope to incorporate in our everyday lives.

We feel more open and spontaneous. This makes us more loving and accepting, and thus more connected with our fellow man. We feel like we are fully functioning, like an engine that suddenly fires on all cylinders and performs perfectly. We feel blessed and grateful for such an experience. In *New Pathways in Psychology: Maslow and the Post-Freudian Revolution,* Colin Wilson writes, "The peak experience induces the recognition that your own powers are far greater than you imagined them."

"There are realms of consciousness still undreamed of, vast ranges of experience, like the humming of unseen harps we know nothing of, within us. Oh when man has escaped from the dark barbed wire entanglement of his own ideas and his own mechanical devices, there is a marvelous rich world of contact and sheer fluid beauty."
—D. H. LAWRENCE

Black browed albatross and chick. Falkland Islands

Maslow believed that peak experiences are transient moments of self-actualization. In fact, his vocabulary for both peak experiences and self-actualization is similar: a sense of wonder, feeling immersed in the present moment, and seeing the world with fresh eyes. The challenge is to transfer those feelings to our daily lives. It is important to reinforce Maslow's point that any of us can have peak experiences, even if we are a long way from self-actualization.

"There are moments in our lives, there are moments in a day, when we seem to see beyond the usual. Such are the moments of our greatest happiness; such are the moments of our greatest wisdom."
—*ROBERT HENRI*

French skier and mountain guide Patrick Vallecant, in his book *Ski Extreme*, writes, "There is something better in us because of our feats in these mountains; we become more at peace with ourselves...my heart is open and free, my head is clear...all the beauty of the world is within the mad rhythm of my blood."

Personal peak experiences

I am grateful to have had peak experiences. On two occasions, I was actually able to photograph the events while they were occurring. Such emotionally meaningful encounters were a powerful motivating force for the creation of this book.

Humpback whales, Antarctica

In January, 2008, I watched a female humpback whale with her calf swimming together off the northern coast of Antarctica. They cruised around, presumably feeding on a swarm of krill, the minute sea animals (similar to shrimp) that are the whale's primary food. Their humps rose to the surface and sank over and over again. Adults average fifty feet in length and thirty-five tons in weight, yet humpbacks are amazingly acrobatic and energetic, and powerful enough to leap completely out of the water. This is called *breeching*.

While I was observing them, the two whales raised their tails above the water together in preparation for a deep dive. Watching those whales with the backdrop of the unspoiled grandeur of Antarctica was exhilarating, but witnessing the moment that mother and calf began their deep dive together in perfect harmony was truly a peak experience.

Humpback whales diving, Antarctica

Zebra and cattle egret. Zambia

Zebra and cattle egret, Zambia

In Zambia, on a 2004 African safari, we came upon a
herd of zebras. Like fingerprints, each zebra's stripes are
unique. In a herd, which might number 150 animals, the
mass of stripes confuses predators. Cattle egrets follow
herds of large grazing animals, such as water buffalo and
zebras, because they stir up grasshoppers and other
insects.

That day, I photographed a cattle egret as it approached a
zebra lit by the afternoon sun. For me, the image was
magical—and it just got better with each step the cattle
egret took. The closer it came to the zebra, the harder my
heart pounded, until it almost exploded out of my chest.
This peak experience resonated deeply within me, to a
great extent because it was a potent symbol of the balance
and interconnectedness in nature.

Limitations of peak experiences

Peak experiences are moments to be treasured. At the
same time, it is important to remember that they are
essentially subjective, and, thus far, science has not been
able to quantify these experiences. We know from history
that inner voices and revelations may be mistaken,
and that delusions can occur as a result of the brain being
functionally impaired by intoxicants or illness.

Abraham Maslow himself expressed the concern that
"out of the joy and wonder of his or her ecstasies,
one might be tempted to seek them out at the expense
of other important aspects of life."

Flow state

It can be challenging to separate the phrases *peak experiences, flow state,* and *in the zone* into different categories. Science has not provided us with the tools to distinguish one from another. Often they are used interchangeably. For example, in *Peak: How Great Companies Get their Mojo from Maslow,* Chip Conley writes, "A peak experience—comparable to being in the zone or in the flow—is when what ought to be just is. Peak experiences are transcendental moments when everything just seems to fit together perfectly. They're very difficult to capture—just like you can't trap a rainbow in a jar." I think of flow state as being related to peak experiences, but being less ethereal in nature.

Cognitive psychologist Mihaly Csikszentmihayli coined the term *flow state* in his book *Finding Flow.* In a state of flow, there is effortless concentration, and all concerns other than the activity in the here and now drop away. He described flow state in the context of work. The flow state renews one's energy rather than drains it. This corroborates Maslow's ideas about narrowing the separation between work and play—a distinction often transcended in the self-actualized. The flow state since has been adapted to other areas besides work, such as sports. A flow state tends to occur when a person faces a clear set of goals and receives immediate results, which is one reason why we love to participate in games and sports. For example, after hitting a shot in golf or in tennis, the consequence is instantaneous.

The flow state also happens when a person's challenges are at a level appropriate to his or her skills. Thus, a person does not have to be an expert to experience this state.

"To burn always with this hard gem-like flame, to maintain this ecstasy is success in life."
—WALTER PATER

In their book, *In The Zone: Transcendent Experience in Sports,* Michael Murphy and Rhea White record many eloquent descriptions of how people felt when they were in the zone. Famed golfer Arnold Palmer, for example, discusses the feelings that he sometimes gets in tournament play. Palmer writes, "There is concentration on the shot at hand, and the heightened sense of presence and renewal that endures through an entire round… There is something spiritual… You're involved in the action and vaguely aware of it, but your focus is not on the commotion but on the opportunity ahead… There is an internal sense of rightness."

Magellanic penguins. Falkland Islands

Basketball star Bill Russell called them "magic moments" in *Bill Russell: A Biography*, by Murry R. Nelson. He recalls states of consciousness in which his concentration was so intense that his play rose to new heights and he could almost predict where the next play would be.

I have been fortunate to have felt the flow state in different arenas, including while seeing patients in the office, performing surgery, playing tennis, and even writing this book. The following example occurred while traveling: While on a bus on Achill Island in the far west of Ireland, just off the coast of County Mayo, I saw a double rainbow. The only thing marring it as a photographic composition was a distracting road in the foreground. When the bus stopped, I ran into the field beyond, so that greenery would be in front of the rainbow in the photograph. Luckily, I had just acquired a fisheye lens, which was necessary to fit the entire rainbow into the image. Everything seemed to move in slow motion. Arriving at the perfect vantage point, solving the technical details of the photograph, and comprehending the majesty of the scene—all seemed to flow together in seamless harmony.

Double rainbow. Achill Island, Ireland

Awe-inspiring experiences

What is awe? In 1757, Edmund Burke defined it in *A Philosophical Inquiry into the Origin of our Ideas of the Sublime and Beautiful* as "the sublime feeling of expanded thought and greatness of mind that is produced by literature, poetry, painting and viewing landscapes." Many of us have, indeed, been inspired by these arts, but certainly we are not limited to them. As with peak experiences, awe-inspiring experiences can bring us more in touch with a sense of the poetry and beauty in our daily lives. I think of awe-inspiring experiences as being related to peak experiences. However, one remains aware of self and place instead of being disconnected from time and space.

Awe-inspiring experiences are available to each of us. So how do we find them? The possibility of beauty and adventure beckons around every corner and can be discovered in our families, friends, teachers, books, work, play, pets, and imaginations. Wondrous experiences can occur when traveling or in one's own backyard.

Autumn leaves. Bannockburn, Illinois

Temple of Poseidon. Sounion, Greece

Personal awe-inspiring experiences

The Temple of Poseidon in Sounion, Greece, was built in 440 B.C.E. by Pericles, at the tip of the Attic peninsula, which juts into the Aegean Sea. To stand at that magnificent place watching the sun set together with three generations of my family and our close friends was sublime.

"The art of architecture studies not structure itself, but the effect of structure on the human spirit."
—GEOFFREY SCOTT

I experienced a similar feeling on two very different days in Spain. On the first, I toured El Castillo Cave, near the town of Puente Viesgo, and viewed cave paintings from 18,000 B.C.E. The following day I visited the Guggenheim Museum in Bilbao. Thus, on successive days, I witnessed two great artistic achievements created 20,000 years apart.

"Every great work of art has two faces, one toward its own time and one toward the future, toward eternity."
—DANIEL BARENBOIM

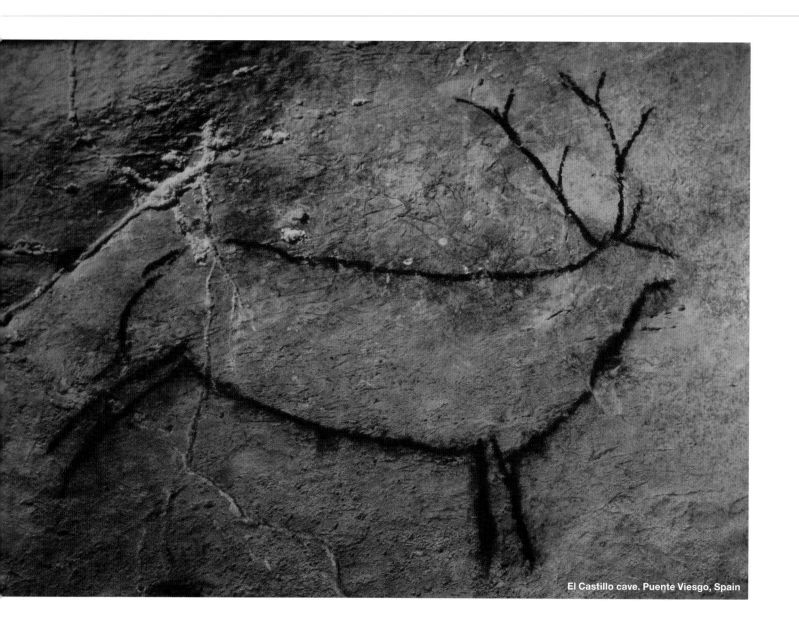

El Castillo cave. Puente Viesgo, Spain

Guggenheim museum. Bilbao, Spain

146

Valerie Lewis and grandson, Cove

Awe-inspiring experiences can occur at home as well. My wife and I are frequently entranced by foxes, coyotes, and deer in our own backyard. In some seasons, Cooper's hawks and great horned owls take up residence nearby. In spring there are visits from Baltimore orioles, bluebirds, ruby-throated hummingbirds, and myriad warblers.

Each of us, even residents of dense urban areas, can avail ourselves of the natural world where awe-inspiring experiences happen daily. One can observe the ever-changing clouds, smell spring blossoms after a long winter, or feel cooling rain on a hot summer's day.

"I stuck my head out of the window this morning and spring kissed me bang in the face."
—*LANGSTON HUGHES*

Then, of course, there are our children and grand-children—wonders to marvel at day after day.

"We find such delight in the beauty and happiness of children that it makes the heart too big for the body."
—*RALPH WALDO EMERSON*

Full circle

In the introduction to this book, I wondered: Why are not more of us in a perpetual state of gratitude? What are the ingredients of a satisfying life? Abraham Maslow's studies of the self-actualized begin to answer these questions. We can emulate the characteristics of the self-actualized. We can choose to shape our own reality, make creative choices, see the extraordinary in the ordinary, laugh and love more. We can adopt a mindset of self-examination, appreciation, and joyful anticipation.

There is a balance between spending time seeking new experiences and reflecting upon previous ones. With profound humility and gratitude, I now spend much more time contemplating the meaning of the varied and rich stories that are my life, and I attempt to share many of them in this book.

*"Each moment has been so slow and so full and
so drenched in sweetness and my life has gone
by so fast."*
—*MARY OLIVER*

Vincent van Gogh, in a letter to his sister Wilhemina van Gogh, writes, "This summer I saw more colors than before." We can all "see more colors"—that is, experience life more fully—by implementing what we have learned from Abraham Maslow. He has given us a path.

Mountain in clouds. Canadian Rockies

Abraham Maslow teaching a class

Appendix One
Brandeis in the 1960s

How can I describe the excitement of attending Brandeis University in the early 1960s? Imagine a small liberal arts college where Leonard Bernstein was the first head of the music department, Eleanor Roosevelt taught international affairs, and guest faculty included Nobel Laureate Martin Luther King, Jr., writer James Baldwin, playwright Lillian Hellman, and composer Aaron Copland.

Abram Sachar, the first president of Brandeis University, was a master recruiter. He had a grand vision and was in a hurry to accomplish it. Remember that Brandeis first came into existence in 1948; the attempt to create a world-class academic institution in a short time was a monumental task. No wonder that one of Sachar's favorite expressions was, "If you are going to leap across a chasm, you had better not do it in two steps."

Leonard Bernstein

Eleanor Roosevelt

One of Sachar's most important decisions was to hire Abraham Maslow. In *The Right to be Human*, Edward Hoffman's biography of Maslow, the author tells the story of Maslow's 1951 job interview for chairman of the soon-to-be-created department of psychology at Brandeis. Maslow was interviewed by an acting dean, history professor Frank Manuel, "who tried an old and effective ruse, in which he fabricated the names of several 'research psychologists' and asked the applicant what he thought of their work. Had Maslow tried to bluff, the interview would likely have ended right there. Maslow humbly replied, "I've never heard of them. What is their research about?" Satisfied with Maslow's integrity, Manuel proceeded to have a lively discussion of ideas."

Once employed, Maslow then set out to create a first-class department of psychology. Hoffman says of Maslow, "He hired bright people who lacked a doctorate and others who had been forced to retire but weren't ready to be put out to pasture." He hired those interested in clinical psychology and those interested in basic laboratory research. Someone else in Maslow's position might have employed people who were concerned with the same kind of academic questions and who thought as he did, but Maslow did not. He simply was interested in building the best possible department.

Brandeis fostered an energetic exchange of ideas. David Hackett Fischer, a Pulitzer Prize-winning historian, recalls that, upon his arrival at the Brandeis campus for an interview, John Roche, a professor of politics and an advisor to John Kennedy and Lyndon Johnson, was arguing vociferously with a colleague over a political difference. Hackett Fischer immediately thought, "This is where I want to be."

Brandeis professors

Arriving at Brandeis without having a fixed direction enabled me to be open to new ideas and directions. I took classes in psychology, philosophy, sociology, history, politics, economics, music, art, theatre, literature, and Spanish, as well as my pre-medical classes. Many other professors greatly expanded my horizons, in addition to Abraham Maslow: Leo Bronstein, Robert Koff, James Klee, Max Lerner, Herbert Marcuse, Louis Kronenberger, and Frank Manuel.

Leo Bronstein

Robert Koff (with wife Rosalind Koff, pianist)

Leo Bronstein was a brilliant art historian, who opened the world of art and artists to me. He helped me to understand how artists express emotion through color and form, which inspired my subsequent interest in photography. Nobel Peace Prize winner Elie Weisel wrote, "To read Leo Bronstein is to discover one of this generation's most original thinkers."

Robert Koff was an original member of the Julliard String Quartet. He taught a course on chamber music, and often played violin-piano duets with his wife in class. "Play as if you were telling a story," he encouraged. His class was pure joy, as he had a boyish enthusiasm for all types of composers, from Joseph Haydn and Wolfgang Amadeus Mozart to Béla Bartók and Arnold Schoenberg.

I had only a rudimentary idea of what chamber music was when I signed up for the class, but I was told that the class was magical, and it was. Thus my best advice to college students: sign up for the professor, not the subject.

James Klee

Max Lerner

James Klee, an associate professor of psychology, taught courses with such titles as *Choice, Will, and the Ego* and *The Psychology of Symbolic Processes*. He was an original thinker who always had fascinating perspectives on wide-ranging subjects, such as man's perception of good and evil and the physical and mental origins of emotions.

Max Lerner, author of the widely read and praised book, *America as a Civilization*, commuted from New York to Boston every week to teach. He also contributed a syndicated column to the *New York Post*, where he wrote, "The so-called lessons of history are for the most part the rationalizations of the victors. History is written by the survivors."

While at Brandeis, he espoused his liberal political and economic views, which included advocating the right of Soviet and eastern European Jews to emigrate to Israel. This was the genesis of my subsequent involvement in the movement to free Refuseniks from the Soviet Union.

Herbert Marcuse

Herbert Marcuse, a member of the politics department, was a self-proclaimed Marxist, socialist, and Hegelian, and author of *Eros and Civilization*. He greatly influenced my fellow students, political activists Angela Davis and Abbie Hoffman.

Frank Manuel

Frank Manuel, one of the most respected European intellectual historians of the twentieth century, enthralled the entire freshman class as he bellowed out his lectures on Jean-Jacques Rousseau, the French Revolution, and Karl Marx.

Louis Kronenberger

Louis Kronenberger, a professor of theatre arts and a drama critic for TIME magazine, also commuted from New York. He not only gave us insight into the plays of Anton Chekhov and George Bernard Shaw but also entertained us with behind-the-scenes tales of producing plays for Broadway.

Brandeis postscript

I began at Brandeis University in 1960. Initially, college life for our class was a continuation of the conservative social norms of the 1950s. Men and women lived in separate dormitories. The women had curfews, and, as freshmen, wore white gloves to the president's tea.

To me, it seemed that most of us were filled with excitement and hope for the future, and we took our studies very seriously. Later, when we became more involved in eastern religions, the civil rights movement, and protesting the Vietnam War, it became clear that we were on the cusp of a cultural revolution.

On November 22, 1963, a cataclysmic event jolted everyone. On that day, I was attending Professor Bronstein's art history class, when someone burst into the room and announced that President John F. Kennedy had been shot in Dallas, Texas.

Brandeis was always at the forefront of cultural and political change, but the pace of that change accelerated after President Kennedy's death. My cousin Alan Waldman enrolled at Brandeis University three years later than I did. Even though our time there overlapped, he paints a very different picture of his college years. There was a stronger anti-authoritarian feeling, more protests, and more drug use. Both of us agree that, for his cohort of students, college life was much more about breaking through the social restraints of the previous age.

Lasting relationships

It has been almost fifty years since I arrived at Brandeis University, and I still feel the influence of my professors on a daily basis. Among my closest friends today are fellow classmates from my freshman year dormitory. We have stayed involved in the events of each other's lives—our own weddings, illnesses, and honors; our children's bar and bat mitzvahs, and their weddings; and, most recently, the pleasures of grandchildren. We continue to vacation together annually. The lasting connections established at Brandeis have added immeasurable richness to my life.

Appendix Two
Teachers, Role Models, Heroes

Henry Fairlie, a twentieth-century British author and journalist, writes, "Heroes remind us of what lies unrecognized and unused in ourselves, and what lies unrecognized and unused in our society." We need teachers, role models, and heroes.

"People seldom improve when they have no model but themselves to copy after."
—OLIVER GOLDSMITH

We often do not realize how much influence role models have on our behavior. For example, many of us in medical school chose a specialty, such as surgery or internal medicine, because a specific physician we admired served as a role model. To me, no particular medical specialty is intrinsically more interesting than another. Rather, I feel that it is the individual practitioners who make one field seem more challenging and appealing than another.

Of course, for many of us, our most important role models are in our immediate family. This is certainly true for me. Another book would be required to attempt to convey their impact adequately.

Here are four non-family members who have been role models for me: two teachers, a professional colleague, and a personal friend.

Mollie Martin

Mollie Martin, my high school debate teacher, set high standards and was exceedingly demanding. Everyone worked on debate assignments for several hours a night and most weekends, in addition to our other homework. As the eminent Harvard biologist E. O. Wilson says in the autobiographical *Naturalist*, "The best of several teachers in my life have been those that told me that my very best was not good enough." So it was with Mollie Martin. She taught us how to think clearly, dissect an argument, and organize our thoughts in a persuasive manner. Most importantly, she instilled in us the ability to see both sides of an issue. Yes, we won numerous speech and debate tournaments. But it is the capacity to see another viewpoint that has become invaluable in subsequent years. I have come to realize that many of us are not born with this ability, and that acquiring it is largely a matter of training.

"It's good to rub and polish your mind against those of others."
—*MICHEL DE MONTAIGNE*

"Who were your most influential teachers?" It is one of my favorite questions to ask other people. Many respond with the name of a high school teacher, or, not infrequently, a junior high school teacher. Pulitzer Prize-winning author Thomas Friedman eulogized his favorite teacher in a *New York Times* column. She taught journalism in the tenth grade. Initially she did not let young Tom into her class because she did not think he was a good enough writer. Friedman describes her classroom as a favorite hang-out for students. Like Mollie Martin, his teacher set high standards and was able to transmit her approach to difficult problems with clarity.

"Teach quality to your students. Quality tends to fan out in waves. Any improvement in the world will come when quality decisions are made."
—*ROBERT PIRSIG*

Besides being in charge of a residency program, he published important scientific papers, had a busy private practice, and led the residency training examination for the American Academy of Orthopedic Surgeons. There are leaders who, from a comfortable distance, command others to go into the battlefield. Henry Mankin led by his actions, not just his words, and to this day continues to inspire a new generation of orthopedic surgeons.

"A teacher affects eternity. He can never tell where his influence will stop."
—HENRY ADAMS

Henry Mankin, Jr., M.D.

Henry Mankin, Jr., M.D., chief of my residency program in orthopedic surgery at Hospital for Joint Diseases in New York City, also had incredibly high standards. For me, he was the epitome of leadership by example. Typically, we arrived at the hospital by five a.m., and finished our rounds in time to meet him for breakfast by seven a.m. We were frequently on call, and were busy in the hospital throughout the day. It was a grueling schedule. What made it possible to bear was that Henry Mankin demanded even more of himself. No matter how early we appeared, he was already there working.

William Meltzer, M.D.

William Meltzer, M.D., has been my mentor, role model, and partner in the practice of orthopedic surgery for more than thirty years. The word that best describes him is professionalism. Like the finest athletes, he "brings his A game" every day. His energy level is legendary; he requires just four hours of sleep each day and does not stop during the other twenty.

My late father, Nathan Lewis, impressed upon me the philosophy that being professional means doing what you love even on the days when you don't feel like doing it. Dad was a business man who, except on one occasion in which he gave himself the luxury of gall bladder surgery, never missed work in more than fifty years. Bill takes the same approach. No one could ever tell by Bill's behavior if he was feeling unwell or was concerned about a family problem. One of Theodore Roosevelt's dictums was, The first requisite of a good citizen is that he shall be able and willing to pull his weight." Bill Meltzer always does more than his share of the work.

Bill was first in his class at university and at medical school. He has only to express his thoughtful opinions on almost any subject to reveal his incisive, laser-like intellect. For many years, a large number of orthopedic surgeons attended a weekly conference at the University of Illinois Medical Center. A case would be presented, and everyone would offer opinions about what should be done. Bill would always be called upon last and would, in my view, consistently contribute the best diagnostic and treatment plans.

His reply? That he was embarrassed that he did not know enough about George Washington and was, therefore, reading several books about him.

"To me old age is ten years older than I am at the time."
—BERNARD BARUCH, AT AGE EIGHTY-FIVE

As chairman of the Mayer and Morris Kaplan Foundation, Morry Kaplan is deeply involved in numerous philanthropic projects, and is a life member of many civic boards. He is constantly thinking about ways to make the world better, and then acting upon those ideas. As an athlete, he once beat Jesse Owens in a broad jumping contest, and he still has a first-rate singing voice. He has a great capacity for friendship and manages to balance myriad interests with time for both family and friends.

The term *elevation* has been coined by Jonathan Haidt, an associate professor of psychology at the University of Virginia. In his book, *The Happiness Hypothesis*, Haidt defines elevation as "an emotional response to moral beauty. It is a warm and pleasant feeling in the chest and a desire to become a better person, or to lead a better life." I feel this about Morry: elevation, admiration and love. He is the whole package: curious, imaginative, kind, a good listener, and passionately dedicated to making the world better. For me, it does not get any better than when a close friend is also one's hero.

Morry Kaplan

Morry Kaplan is who I want to be like when I grow up. He introduced me into a book club that consists of eleven men and has been in existence for more than forty years. At book club, he frequently regales us with personal experiences he has had with the authors and prominent individuals about whom we are reading—in addition to offering up cogent comments on the work itself. Now in his mid-nineties, Morry never stops expanding his mind. I recently asked him which book he was reading.

Sources

This section contains a list of the primary sources I have used in this book. It is not meant to be a detailed bibliography.

Books written by Abraham Maslow include *Motivation and Personality; Religions, Values, and Peak Experiences; The Farther Reaches of Human Nature; Toward a Psychology of Being;* and *Maslow on Management* (with commentary and contributions by Deborah C. Stephens and Gary Heil).

Books edited by Abraham Maslow include *New Knowledge in Human Values.*

Books about Abraham Maslow include *The Right to be Human: a Biography of Abraham Maslow* by Edward Hoffman; *The Journals of Abraham Maslow* edited by Richard Lowry; *Future Visions: The Unpublished Papers of Abraham Maslow* edited by Edward Hoffman; *The Third Force: The Psychology of Abraham Maslow* by Frank G. Goble; *New Pathways in Psychology: Maslow and the Post-Freudian Revolution* by Colin Wilson; and *Peak: How Great Companies Get Their Mojo from Maslow* by Chip Conley.

Video interviews with Abraham Maslow include: *Being Abraham Maslow* with Warren Bennis and *Maslow and Self-Actualization* with Dr. Everett Shostrom.

Maslow's ideas have strongly influenced how business management is taught. Books I have read by business consultants who have acknowledged their debt to Maslow include *The Frontiers of Management* by Peter F. Drucker, *On Becoming a Leader* by Warren Bennis, and *Principle-Centered Leadership* by Stephen R. Covey.

In order to better understand Abraham Maslow's academic predecessors I have read *The Interpretation of Dreams, The Ego and The Id,* and *Civilization and its Discontents* by Sigmund Freud, the scientific papers of Harry Harlow, and *Science and Human Behavior* and *Walden Two,* by B. F. Skinner.

Books of related interest by Abraham Maslow's contemporaries include *Man's Search for Meaning* by Viktor E. Frankl, *Becoming* by Gordon W. Allport, *Love and Will* by Rollo May, *The Art of Loving* by Erich Fromm, and *A Way of Being* by Carl R. Rogers.

Abraham Maslow's revolutionary idea of formulating a theory of personality based on studying the mentally healthy has spawned an entire movement called positive psychology. These authors have increased my understanding of what might lead to a more satisfying life. Jonathan Haidt in *The Happiness Hypothesis,* Martin E. P. Seligman in *Authentic Happiness,* Corey L. M. Keyes in *Flourishing: Positive Psychology and the Life Well-Lived,* David G. Myers in *The Pursuit of Happiness,* Sonja Lyubomirsky in *The How of Happiness,* Lisa G. Aspinwall in *A Psychology of Human Strengths: Fundamental Questions and Future Directions for a Positive Psychology,* Ed Diener and Robert Biswas-Diener in *Happiness: Unlocking the Mysteries of Psychological Wealth.*

Psychology professor Tal Ben-Shahar teaches the most popular undergraduate course at Harvard University. These teachings can be found in his recent books: *Happier, The Pursuit of Perfect,* and *Even Happier.*

Gregg Easterbrook in his book *The Progress Paradox* discusses the reasons for our lack of satisfaction in an age of abundance. Daniel Gilbert articulates many misconceptions concerning happiness in *Stumbling on Happiness.*

Historically travel has stimulated people's imaginations, and travelers have been writing for centuries about their adventures. Travel books I recommend include *The Histories* by Herodotus, *The Travels of Marco Polo: the Venetian* by Marco Polo, *Democracy in America* by Alexis de Tocqueville, *The Innocents Abroad* by Mark Twain, *Down and Out in Paris and London* by George Orwell, *The White Nile* and *The Blue Nile* by Alan Moorehead, *Endurance: Shackleton's Incredible Voyage* by Alfred Lansing, *In Patagonia* and *The Songlines* by Bruce Chatwin, *The Great Railway Bazaar* and *Dark Star Safari: Overland from Cairo to Capetown* by Paul Theroux, *In a Sunburned Country* by Bill Bryson, and *The Places in Between* by Rory Stewart.

Many authors have written enlightening accounts of their travels across America in search of wisdom and themselves. These include *Life on the Mississippi* by Mark Twain, *Blue Highways* by William Least Heat-Moon, *Zen and the Art of Motorcycle Maintenance* by Robert M. Pirsig, and *What Really Matters* by Tony Schwartz.

The works of Abraham Joshua Heschel and Elie Wiesel have added to my understanding of Jewish philosophical traditions. My religious knowledge has been enhanced by Rabbis Hyman Judah Schachtel, Samuel Dresner, and Samuel Fraint. In the 1960s, "eastern religions" were in vogue, and I read many Hindu, Buddhist, and Zen Buddhist texts, including the *Bhagavad Gita, The Tibetan Book of Living and Dying* by Sogyal Rinpoche, and the works of D. T. Suzuki, Alan Watts, and more recently, Ken Wilbur and Jon Kabat-Zinn.

Abraham Maslow's interest in peak experiences fostered an interest in mystical experiences. William James describes such experiences in many different religious traditions in *The Varieties of Religious Experience.* Arthur Schopenhauer in *The World as Will and Representation* discusses the possibility of absolute knowledge by means of mystical experience. Peak experiences in sports are beautifully articulated in *In the Zone: Transcendent Experience in Sports* by Michael Murphy and Rhea A. White. The flow state is discussed by Mihaly Csikszentmihalyi in *Finding Flow.*

My ideas of creativity and forms of intelligence have been expanded by Howard Gardner in *Frames of Mind: The Theory of Multiple Intelligences* and *Art, Mind and Brain: A Cognitive Approach to Creativity,* Daniel Goleman in *Emotional Intelligence,* Robert J. Sternberg in *Successful Intelligence,* Antonio Damasio in *Descartes' Error,* and Jonah Lehrer in *How We Decide.*

Many books have been written on techniques to increase one's creativity. I have found these helpful: *Whole-Brain Thinking* by Jacquelyn Wonder and Priscilla Donovan, *The Mind Map Book* by Tony Buzan, *The Creative Spirit* by Daniel Goleman, Paul Kaufman, and Michael Ray, and *Drawings on the Right Side of the Brain* by Betty Edwards.

The importance of self-reliance and of shaping our own destinies are central themes in the writings of Henry David Thoreau, Ralph Waldo Emerson, and Benjamin Franklin. Wallace Stevens, the twentieth-century American poet, has further articulated the idea that we create our own reality and that we are capable of envisioning paradise here on earth.

Thoughts on friendship were influenced by Plato's ideas of universal forms, Aristotle's essays on ethics, the writings of Ralph Waldo Emerson, *Philosophical Explanations* by Robert Nozick, and *The Moral Animal* by Robert Wright.

The late Eli Segal and Geoffrey Tabin, M.D., are two friends of mine mentioned in this book because of their contributions to society. Some of their accomplishments are discussed in *Common Interest Common Good: Creating Value through Business and Social Sector Partnerships* by Shirley Sagawa and Eli Segal and *Blind Corners* by Geoffrey Tabin, M.D.

Books which have deepened my understanding of the natural world include *On the Origin of Species* and *The Expression of the Emotions in Man and Animals*, by Charles Darwin, *Silent Spring* by Rachel Carson, *A Neotropical Companion* by John Kricher, *Tropical Nature* by Adrian Forsyth and Ken Miyata, *In the Rainforest* by Catherine Caufield, *Beautiful Swimmers* by William W. Warner, *The Sibley Guide to Bird Life and Behavior* by David Allen Sibley, *Tales of A Shaman's Apprentice* by Mark J. Plotkin, *The Panda's Thumb, Hen's Teeth and Horse's Toes*, and *Ever Since Darwin* by Stephen Jay Gould, *On Human Nature* and *Consilience* by Edward O. Wilson, *Coming into the Country* by John McPhee, *Arctic Dreams* and *Crossing Open Ground* by Barry Lopez, *Desert Solitaire* by Edward Abbey, *The Natural History of the Senses* by Diane Ackerman, and *Pilgrim at Tinker Creek* by Annie Dillard.

Books related to our impact on the economic, political, and environmental future of our planet include *Guns, Germs, and Steel* and *Collapse* by Jared Diamond, *The Lexus and the Olive Tree, The World is Flat* and *Hot, Flat and Crowded* by Thomas L. Friedman, *The Big Necessity* by Rose George, *Massive Change* by Bruce Mau, and *The End of Poverty* by Jeffrey D. Sachs.

Books by and about writers, artists, and scientists include *A Writer's Notebook* by Somerset Maugham, *An American Childhood* and *The Writing Life* by Annie Dillard, *Bird by Bird* by Anne Lamott, *Jack London: Sailor on Horseback* by Irving Stone, *Genius* by Harold Bloom, *The Art Spirit* by Robert Henri, *A Life of Picasso* by John Richardson, *Surely you're joking, Mr. Feynman!* by Richard Feynman, *Genome* by Matt Ridley, and *Einstein* by Walter Isaacson.

I have read collections of the writings of each of the poets quoted in this book, as well as the complete works of Pablo Neruda and Rumi. A list of all of the works of fiction which have influenced this book is a subject for another project.

I have collected quotations for the past fifty years from reading the primary sources of those who are quoted, and from collections of quotations, including multiple readings of *Bartlett's Familiar Quotations* and the *Yale Book of Quotations*.

Books specifically referred to in this volume include *Principles of Abnormal Psychology* by Abraham Maslow and Bela Mittelmann, *Motivation and Personality* by Abraham Maslow, *The Writing Life* by Annie Dillard, *The Art Spirit* by Robert Henri, *The Future of the Body: Explorations into the Further Evolution of Human Nature* by Michael Murphy, *Who Is Man?* by Abraham Joshua Heschel, *The 7 Habits of Highly Effective People* by Stephen Covey, *Colored People* by Henry Louis Gates, Jr., *Unfair Advantage* by Tom Miller, *Fear No Evil* by Anatoly Sharansky, *Wisdom, Intelligence and Creativity Synthesized* by Robert J. Sternberg, *Multiple Intelligences: New Horizons in Theory and Practice* by Howard Gardner, *Emotional Intelligence* by Daniel Goleman, *The Creative Spirit* by Daniel Goleman, Paul Kaufman, and Michael Ray, *Sacred Hoops* by Phil Jackson, *Fly Fishing through the Midlife Crisis* by Howell Raines, *Wherever You Go, There You Are* by Jon Kabat-Zinn, *No Matter What!* by Lisa Nichols, *Soul Stories* by Gary Zukav, *The Cultural Animal: Human Nature, Meaning and Social Life* by Roy F. Baumeister, *Walden* by Henry David Thoreau, *The Pursuit of Happiness* by David G. Myers,

Against Silence: The Voice and Vision of Elie Wiesel edited by Irving Abrahamson, *My Old Man and the Sea* by David Hayes and Daniel Hayes, *Veeck as in Wreck* by Bill Veeck, *The How of Happiness* by Sonja Lyubomirsky, *Here at the New Yorker* by Brendan Gill, *Man's Search for Meaning* by Viktor E. Frankl, *Predictably Irrational* by Dan Ariely, *The Sacred and the Profane* by Mircea Eliade, *Embracing Earth: New Views of Our Changing Planet* by Payson R. Stevens, *The World as Will and Representation* by Arthur Schopenhauer, *Three Essays of the Theory of Sexuality* by Sigmund Freud, *Rumi, the Path of Love* by Manuela Dunn Mascetti, *100 Love Sonnets* by Pablo Neruda, *Tuesdays with Morrie* by Mitch Albom, *The Seven Principles for Making Marriage Work* by John Gottman, *A Life for a Life* by Dinah Craik, *War and Peace* by Leo Tolstoy, *The Varieties of Religious Experience* by William James, *New Pathways in Psychology: Maslow and the Post-Freudian Revolution* by Colin Wilson, *Ski Extreme* by Patrick Vallecant; *Peak: How Great Companies Get their Mojo from Maslow* by Chip Conley, *In the Zone: Transcendent Experience in Sports* by Michael Murphy and Rhea A. White, *Bill Russell: A Biography* by Murry R. Nelson, *A Philosophical Enquiry into the Origin of our Ideas of the Sublime and Beautiful* by Edmund Burke, *Eros and Civilization* by Herbert Marcuse, *The Right to be Human* by Edward Hoffman, *America as a Civilization* by Max Lerner, *Naturalist* by E. O. Wilson, and *The Happiness Hypothesis* by Jonathan Haidt.

About
Michael S. Lewis, M.D.

Michael S. Lewis, M.D., has published *One World, A View of Seven Continents*, an award-winning book featured on PBS-TV. In addition, he has collaborated on *Eagle Eyes*, a children's book written by *New York Times* best-selling author Jacquelyn Mitchard, which contains his photographs. His images have been published in a number of other books and magazines, including the *Field Museum of Natural History Bulletin, Nature Photographer, Living City Magazine, North Shore Magazine,* and *B & W Contest Awards Special Issue.*

His photographs have been shown in several galleries and exhibitions, including Brandeis University in Waltham, Massachusetts; the Moscone Convention Center in San Francisco, California; the Chicago Cultural Center in Chicago, Illinois; Ryerson Nature Center, Deerfield, Illinois; and Children's Hospital of Harvard University, Boston, Massachusetts.

Dr. Lewis is an orthopedic surgeon at the Illinois Bone and Joint Institute. He has been chief of staff at Rush North Shore Medical Center, and received a best teacher award from Rush Medical School. Additionally, he has been an orthopedic consultant to the Chicago White Sox baseball team, the Chicago Wolves hockey team, and the Chicago Bulls basketball team, with whom he earned two championship rings. An avid tennis player, he has won U.S.T.A. Greater Chicagoland singles tournaments. He is married to Valerie Dewar Searle Lewis.

His website is *michaelslewismd.com.*

Praise for the book
One World: A View of Seven Continents

"Michael Lewis is a gifted artist who was born with the true photographer's eye—a rarity in anyone, much less a celebrated pro in another field."
—Art Shay
Veteran Time-Life photojournalist and author/
photographer of 62 books

"Michael's work touches me. He has created magical timeless moments, full of joy and wonder that deserve careful and caring attention. His consistent way of seeing speaks to his love of all things on this planet. He embraces the world, One World."
—John Weiss
Former apprentice to Minor White and former
Professor of Art and Coordinator of Photography,
University of Delaware

"What a powerful and wonderful experience it is to be taken on this fabulous global trip. I felt that I was witness to many 'sacred moments' and I was with you all the way. This book lifted my spirits."
—John Callaway
PBS-TV journalist